KU-661-243

Tracing Your
West Indian
Ancestors

Sources in the
Public Record Office

WITHDRAWN

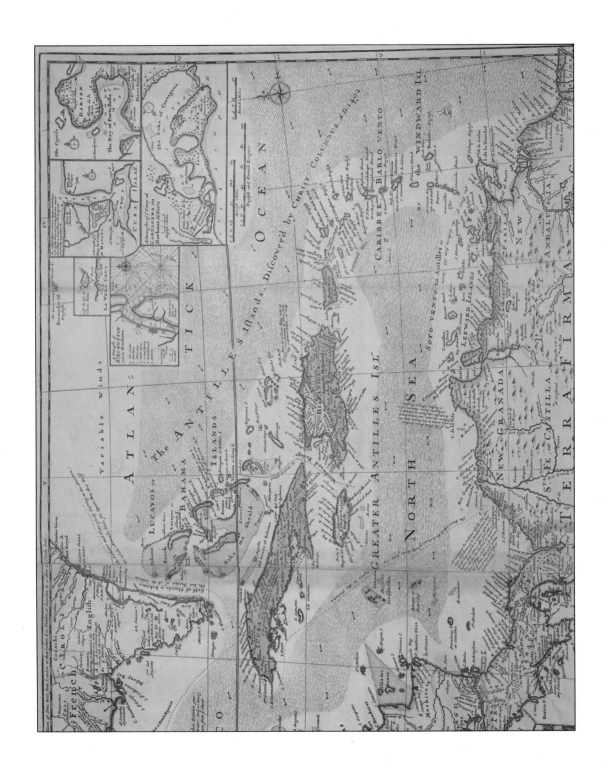

Detail from a map of the West Indies, c.1710. (CO 700 West Indies no 5)

PRO Readers' Guide No 11

Tracing Your West Indian Ancestors

Sources in the Public Record Office

by

Guy Grannum

PRO Publications

PRO Publications
Public Record Office
Chancery Lane
London
WC2A 1LR
A catalogue card for this book is available from the British Library.

© Crown Copyright 1995

ISBN 1 873162 20 0

Contents

Illustrations

General Information about the Public Record Office

At present the records held by the Public Record Office (PRO) are divided between two sites, at Kew and Chancery Lane. Unless otherwise described in this guide are held at Kew. In 1996 the Chancery Lane building will close and all original records will be housed at Kew.

Public Record Office, Ruskin Avenue, Kew, Surrey TW9 4DU.

Public Record Office, Chancery Lane, London WC2A 1LR.

The Office is open from 9.30 am to 5.00 pm Monday to Friday. The Census Rooms are also open from 9.30 am to 5.00 pm on Saturdays.You do not need to make an appointment. Closed on public holidays and for annual stocktaking (usually the first two weeks in October). Museum and Shop open 9.30 am to 4.45 pm. Telephone 0181-876 3444.

When you first visit the PRO, please bring with you formal documentary proof of identity bearing your name and signature. If you are not a British citizen you will need to bring your passport or national identity card. You will then be issued with a Reader's Ticket. Without a valid Reader's Ticket you cannot be admitted to the reading rooms or order documents. You do not need one to visit the Census Rooms or the Museum at Chancery Lane.

You may use only graphite pencils in the reading rooms. Pens of any kind are not allowed. You may use personal computers, typewriters and tape recorders in most of the reading rooms. For a full list of Reading Room rules, please ask for General Information Leaflet no 27: *Rules for Readers*.

Each document has a unique three part reference. The first part is the lettercode, for example CO for the Colonial Office, BT for the Board of Trade, and PC for the Privy Council, according to the department which created it. The second part is the class number, which represents the series within the lettercode; these often equate to types of documents, for example musters, government gazettes or correspondence. The third, and final part, is the piece number, which represents the individual document. For example, the description book for those who enlisted into the 5th West India Regiment, 1811-1817, is WO 25/656, and the 1951 electoral register for Barbados is CO 32/124.

To identify the lettercode and class, consult the Current Guide, which is the primary guide to the holdings of the PRO. The Current Guide is in three parts. Part 1 describes the history and functions of government departments. Part 2 briefly describes each class with information such as the covering dates and number of pieces. Part 3 is the index to the other two parts. There is no general index to records in the PRO. Once possible classes have been identified, the next step is to go to the class lists which briefly describe each piece.

Acknowledgements

I would like to thank Mandy Banton, Margaret Brennand, Karen Cushion, Alfred Knightbridge, James Murray and Melvyn Stainton for their help and advice in the production of this Readers' Guide.

Cover design by Melvyn Stainton.

Chapter 1: Introduction

Much has been written on family history for most of the former British Empire, especially South Africa, Canada, the United States of America, New Zealand and Australia. Very little has been written about the British West Indies, and the other British colonies in Central and South America. The British West Indies are among a chain of islands spreading from Florida to Venezuela. They contain a diverse population of native American Indians, and the descendants of Dutch, Spanish, African, British, Portuguese, Danish, Swedish and French settlers. This small group of islands was important to the development of Britain's empire during the sixteenth to eighteenth centuries. The wealth created by the plantations encouraged the banking and insurance industries, and it is said, sparked Britain's industrial revolution.

The Public Record Office (PRO) holds numerous references to people who lived in the West Indies, such as adventurers who planted sugar cane, slaves who toiled the land, soldiers and sailors who fought in the Napoleonic Wars, transported criminals, and Indians who emigrated as indentured labourers. This Readers' Guide is aimed at research in the British crown colonies and former colonies of Antigua, Bahamas, Barbados, Bermuda, Cayman Islands, Dominica, Grenada, Jamaica, Montserrat, Nevis, St Christopher (St Kitts), St Lucia, St Vincent, Tobago, Trinidad, Turks and Caicos Islands, and the British Virgin Islands, together with Guyana (formerly British Guiana), and Belize (formerly British Honduras). At various times the British also occupied islands held by other European powers, and the records may contain information about their inhabitants. I have included the records of Sierra Leone, which administered many of the territories on the West Coast of Africa, because of the importance of West Africa in the history, people and development of the West Indies.

This Readers' Guide is not intended to be a guide to general genealogical sources and techniques, nor is it meant to stand on its own. I have included a select bibliography at the end of each chapter and noted relevant PRO Records Information leaflets and sections from *Tracing Your Ancestors in the Public Record Office*, 4th edition by Amanda Bevan and Andrea Duncan (London, HMSO, 1990). The leaflets can be obtained in person from the PRO; they will not be sent by post.

The study of genealogy in the West Indies relies on the same sources as used in Britain: parish records; legal records; military service; census returns; tax returns; wills; maps; private correspondence; and newspapers. However, most records suitable for family research, such as church records and wills, are to be found in the archives of the islands.

Before you begin your family history it is important to get as much information as possible from surviving members of your family as to the island of origin. 'My grandfather was born in the West Indies', is not specific enough.

It is important to note that the PRO does not hold the domestic records of colonial governments. These remain with the colony, and may be found in the former colony's archives. Appendix 3 contains the addresses of most of the islands' archives. The PRO holds the records of central government and the courts of law of England and Wales. These are the official records created by British government departments, dating from the Domesday Book in 1086 to the present day. Most records are closed for thirty years, for example a file with papers dating no later than 1964 will not become open until 1995. There are exceptions to this rule: for example, published material is often opened on arrival; while documents which refer to individuals are often closed for longer periods, of up to one hundred years.

General genealogical guides

Chapman, Colin, *Tracing Your British Ancestors* (Lochin Publishing, 1993).

Cole, Jean A and Armstrong, Michael, *Tracing your Family Tree. The Complete Guide to Discovering Your Family History* (London: Guild Publishing, 1988).

Colwell, Stella, *The Family History Book. How to Trace Your Ancestors*, 2nd edn (Oxford, Phaidon Press Ltd, 1989).

Davis, Bill, *An Introduction to Irish Research. Irish Ancestry: a Beginner's Guide* (Federation of Family History Societies, 1992).

Family Tree Magazine, 61 Great Whyte, Ramsey, Huntingdon, Cambridgeshire, PE17 1HL.

FitzHugh, Terrick V H, *The Dictionary of Genealogy. A Guide to British Ancestry Research* (Sherborne, Alphabooks, 1985).

Genealogists' Magazine, Society of Genealogists, 14 Charterhouse Buildings, Goswell Rd, London EC1M 7BA.

Harvey, Richard, *Genealogy for Librarians* (London, Clive Bingley, 1983).

McCarthy, Tony, *The Irish Roots Guide* (Dublin, Lilliput Press, 1991).

Pelling, George, *Beginning Your Family History*, 5th edn (Federation of Family History Societies, 1990).

Philipps, M C and R D, *Family History Research. A Guide to 19th & 20th Century Sources in England and Wales* (London, Certificates & Searches Ltd, 1992).

Scottish Record Office, *Tracing Your Scottish Ancestors* (Edinburgh, HMSO, 1993).

Todd, Andrew, *Basic Record Keeping for Family Historians: An Antidote to Chaos...and No Computers!* (Lancashire, Allen and Todd, 1991).

Todd, Andrew, *Basic Sources for Family History. 1: Back to the Early 1800s* (Lancashire, Allen and Todd, 1989).

Some general genealogical guides to the Public Record Office

Colwell, Stella, *Dictionary of Genealogical Sources in the Public Record Office* (London, Weidenfeld and Nicolson, 1992).

Colwell, Stella, *Family Roots. Discovering the Past in the Public Record Office* (London, Weidenfeld and Nicolson, 1991).

Cox, Jane and Padfield, Timothy, *Tracing Your Ancestors in the Public Record Office*, 4th edn by Amanda Bevan and Andrea Duncan, PRO handbook no 19 (London, HMSO, 1990).

Cox, Jane, *Never Been Here Before? A First Time Guide for Family Historians at the Public Record Office*, PRO readers' guide no 4 (London, PRO Publications, 1993).

Chapter 2: West Indians

When the West Indies were first discovered by Europeans at the end of the fifteenth century, most of the islands had indigenous populations. The Portuguese and Spanish enslaved many of these Indians to work on their plantations and gold mines in South America. Many more were wiped out through disease and invasion. Some Amerindians still survive in the Caribbean, such as in Dominica, but most did not survive European settlement.

The Americas were 'beyond the line', they lay outside the territorial limits of European treaties, and disputes in the Americas did not invalidate peace treaties in Europe. While the Spanish attempted to keep other European powers out of America, the gold of the Spanish Main acted as a lure to adventurers and pirates. Throughout the sixteenth and seventeenth centuries the Spanish gradually lost their hold on the Caribbean and Latin and North America. The Portuguese settled in Brazil, the French and English colonized fragments of North America and many of the West Indian islands, and the Dutch settled Surinam and some islands, and enjoyed a brief spell in Brazil. The Danes and Swedes also colonized some of the islands.

Regular territorial disputes and European wars meant that islands frequently changed hands from one power to another. On islands captured by Britain from the Spanish, French and Dutch, there was little or no attempt to expel all the non-British. During the French Revolution and the Spanish American independence wars many refugees fled to 'friendly' British islands. These non-British populations would also have had their slaves and servants. It is important to realize that as many of the colonies changed hands records may also survive in other European archives. For example, British Guiana was originally Dutch; Jamaica was Spanish; Tobago was at various times occupied by the British, Dutch, French and Germans (Courlanders); and for eighty years St Christopher was jointly shared by both Britain and France.

Labour was necessary for the settled islands to prosper and many thousands, free and unfree, were transported from Europe. From the 1650s the most significant change in the populations was the mass transportation of slave labour from the West Coast of Africa. The Spanish and Portuguese were already using African labour in Latin America, but the numbers enslaved escalated once the Dutch, French and British islands realised the necessity of a large unskilled work force, used to tropical climate, food and diseases to maintain their plantations. It has been estimated that over eleven million Africans were transported to the New World, about 1.6 million slaves to the British West Indies. By the mid-1700s most of the British islands had black populations which far exceeded the white population. It is not possible to identify the origin of the black populations as very poor records were kept, and even where tribal origins are noted these are often the names of the areas of departure from Africa, rather than the true ethnic group.

When slavery was abolished in the British colonies many colonies, notably Trinidad and British Guiana, suffered severe labour problems. Trinidad had established various schemes before 1834 to encourage labour, such as the immigration of Chinese labourers in 1806. Other people encouraged to settle were disbanded soldiers from the West India Regiments; black colonial marines who enlisted in America during the War of 1812; East Indians (from India); Liberated Africans freed from illegal slavers; and Portuguese from Madeira and the Azores.

Further reading:

Curtin, Philip D, *The Atlantic Slave Trade. A Census* (University of Winsconsin Press, 1969).

Dunn, Richard S, *Sugar and Slaves. The Rise of the Planter Class in the English West Indies, 1624-1713* (New York, W W Norton & Company, 1973).

Edwards, Bryan, *The History of the British West Indies*, 5th edn, 5 vols (London, 1819).

Fage, J D, *A History of Africa* (London, Hutchinson, 1986).

Lovejoy, Paul E, *Transformations in Slavery. A History of Slavery in Africa* (Cambridge University Press, 1983).

Lucas, C P, *Historical Geography of the British Colonies, Volume 2, the West Indies* (Oxford, Clarendon Press, 1890).

Chapter 3: Records of the Colonial Office

The most important series of records for the study of West Indian genealogy are those of the Colonial Office and its predecessors. The term 'Colonial Office' as used in this guide refers to the various departments which at different times had oversight of the colonies. These include the various secretaries of state, the Lords of Trade and Plantations, the Board of Trade, various committees of the Privy Council, and the Colonial Office. You should refer to Anne Thurston, *Sources for Colonial Studies in the Public Record Office, I:Records of the Colonial Office, Dominions Office, Commonwealth Relations Office and Commonwealth Office* (London, HMSO, 1995), and the *Public Record Office Current Guide*, Part 1, section 803, for a full description on the history, and the records, of the Colonial Office.

The records of the Colonial Office relating to individual colonies are arranged according to the type of document: original correspondence; entry books; acts; sessional papers; government gazettes; miscellanea; registers of correspondence; and registers of out-letters.

Appendix 1 lists the Colonial Office classes for each colony.

3.1 Original Correspondence

These are letters (despatches) received by the Colonial Office from the governor and other bodies concerning a particular colony. Until 1951 each colony or administrative unit has a separate original correspondence class. Until 1800 the correspondence is arranged by date. From 1801 to 1926 the volumes are arranged firstly by the governor's despatches, then by letters from government departments, and finally by letters from individuals. From 1926 they are in subject files.

Published means of reference into these records is by the *Calendars of State Papers, Colonial, America and West Indies*, 1574-1738, and *Journals of the Board of Trade and Plantations*, 1704-1782. Selected correspondence is described in Lowell Joseph Ragatz, *A Guide to the Official Correspondence of the Governors of the British West India Colonies with the Secretary of*

	Names	Sex	Residence	Colour	age	weekly allowance	Total
1	Baillie John B	Male	BlackGrounds	white	71	13/4	22 13 4
2	Barclay Charles	do	do	do	21	10/	27 – –
3	Barron Emma	Female	Falmouth	Black	71	6/8	17 6 8
4	Benham Thomas	Male	do	mulatto	31	6/8	17 – –
5	Booker Ann	Female	do	do	41	10/	36 – –
6	Burnet Joan F	do	Duncans	white	71	1.5 pan	50 – –
7	Bradly Mary Ann	do	RioBueno	do	41	20/	65 – –
8	Booker Margaret	do	Falmouth	mulatto	41	5/	13 –
9	Buchanan Mary	do	Rock	white	66	4/	23 10 –
10	Brown John	Male	Falmouth	samb.	55	6/8	4 6 8
11	Clark Joan	Female	do	mulatto	36	6/8	17 6 8
12	Colvall Harry	Male	Duncans	Black	41	5/	1 10
13	Crozier Catherine	Female	Falmouth	white	31	40/	104 – –
14	Downer Elizabeth	do	do	mulatto	56	6/8	17 6 8
15	Darcy Ann	do	do	do	41	13/9	34 16 3
16	Dickson Joshua	Male	do	white	48	1.5 pan	10 – –
17	Fergus Mary, 3 children of	—	do	mulatto	19	20/	52 – –
18	Gardner Sarah	Female	do		45	6/8	17 – –
19	Gale Flora	do	do	Black	66	5/	9 15 –
20	Grice Ann	do	do	white	71	13/4	34 13 4
21	Graham Ann M	do	Martha Brae	do	66	8.5 p/mo	50 – –
22	Gallimore Elizth	do	Falmouth	mulatto	71	6/8	17 6 8
23	Gayner Mary	do	do	do	36	6/8	17 6 8
24	Gibson Mary Ann	do	Halfmoon Bay	white	36	1.5 pan	166 13 4
25	Grant Elizabeth	do	Falmouth	mulatto	25	10/	11 10 –
26	Harris Sarah	do	Rock	white	36	13/4	36 – –
27	James Jr Edward	Male	Martha Brae	do	66	13/4	34 13 4
28	Love Isaac	do	Falmouth	mulatto	40	–	13 4
29	McSherry Richard	do	Falmouth	mulatto	31	6/8	6 13 4
30	O'Brien Martha	Female	do	white	26	13/4	19 – –
31	Pugh Mary	do	Martha Brae	do	81	13/4	34 13 4
32	Perry Mary Ann	do	Falmouth	do	71	13/4	8 – –
33	Pigeon Henrietta	do	do	mulatto	41	10/	2 10 –
34	Palmer Elizabeth	do	do	Black	63	5/	11 15 –
35	Penny Susan	do	Falmouth	mulatto	31	10/	26 – –
36	Price Mary	do	do	Black	56	5/	5 – –
37	Rigby Jane	do	Martha Brae	do	66	5/	13 –
38	Shuttleworth Elizth	do	Rock	white	66	40/	25 10 –
39	Stoddart Elizth	do	Falmouth	mulatto	42	6/8	3 6 8
40	Thorburn George	Male	do	white	51	20/	52 – –
41	Vansee Mary	Female	do	do	42	10/	22 10 –
42	Williams Mary	do	do	mulatto	65	13/4	3 6 8
43	Williams Elizth	do	do	Black	71	5/	5 8 –
						Total	1076 17 11

James Sheddle Secretary

Figure 1 Jamaica: return of payments to paupers, December 1823 - December 1824. (CO 137/162, March)

State, 1763-1833. Unpublished reference is through the registers of correspondence which are described in section 3.7.

The papers are predominantly of an official and administrative nature. The following types of records are found, and although they do not occur for every colony, they give an idea of the usefulness of these records: petitions; tax lists; inhabitants lists, which normally give only the name of the household head with the numbers of women, children, servants, and slaves; colonial civil servants' application forms, and pension papers; land grants; newspapers, which sometimes give announcements of births, marriages and deaths; lists of prisoners; and records of the local courts, such as courts of chancery and petty sessions (*see* figure 1).

3.2 Entry Books

These record outgoing correspondence from the Colonial Office to governors, and government departments. They also contain instructions, petitions, letters, reports, and commissions, and include details of patents for grants of land. Before 1700 these record letters received as well as letters despatched. Entry books were superseded in 1872 by the registers of out-letters (section 3.8).

3.3 Acts

These are copies of local acts and ordinances. They include private acts of naturalization in the colony.

3.4 Sessional Papers

These are the proceedings of the executive and legislative councils, which formed the government of each colony. They also contain departmental reports.

3.5 Government Gazettes

These are official newspapers produced by most colonies. Early gazettes were, along with newspapers, the only way the local populations could keep up with the events in Europe, such as wars, royal affairs, and proceedings of Parliament.

6

Christian and Surname.	Place of Abode.	Nature of Qualification.	Place where the property is situate. Name of the property or other description. Name of Tenant &c.
Choppin James Clement	Sion Lodge	Freehold	St. George's Village, Akers Hill
Clinker Edward	Reily's Village	...	Reily's Village
Cox Edward	Stubbs Village	...	Stubbs Village
Cupid John	Evesham Village	...	Evesham Village
David George	Victoria Village	...	Victoria Village
Dick Robert	...	...	...
Douglas Alexander	...	...	...
Edwards John George	Calliaqua	...	Calliaqua, Lot No. 23
Edwards Jackson	Reily's Village	...	Reily's Village
Flockton Webster	Villa Estate	...	St. Georges Parish, Villa Estate
Fraser Thomas	Mustique	...	Calliaqua Point
Griffin Robert	Evesham-Vale Es.	Freehold	Freeland Cottage
Griffin Gilbert	Nutmeg Grove	...	...
Hagart James McCaul	Belvidere Estate	...	St. George's Parish, Belvidere
Henry William	Stubbs Village	...	Stubbs Village
Huggins Robert	Gomea	Leasehold	Gomea Valley, Pilgrim
Hannibal Daniel	Calliaqua	Freehold	Calliaqua
Jack Alexander	Victoria Village	...	Stubbs Village
James Gorgeous James	Calliaqua	...	Calliaqua
Johnson Benjamin	Stubbs Village	...	Stubbs Village
John Diamond	Calder Ridge	...	...
Joseph William	Victoria Village	...	Victoria Village
Joseph Anthony	Reily's Village	...	Reily's Village
John Peter	New Prospect	...	...
Laborde Edward	Kingstown	...	Gomea Valley, Dauphine
London William	Choppin Village	...	Choppin Village
Maule Charles	Stubbs Village	...	Stubbs and Victoria Villages
McLean Joseph	Victoria Village	...	...
Miguel Manoel	Mesopotamia	...	Mesopotamia
Parsons William	Lower Diamond	...	Mesopotamia Valley, Hopewell
Parsons John	Calder Estate	...	Marriaqua Valley, Cariere
Pompey Rambler	Stubbs Village	...	Stubbs Village
Porter David Kennedy	Kingstown	...	St. George's Parish, Lower Diamond
Prince Abraham	Stubbs Village	...	Stubbs Village
Pitcairn William	Brighton Village	...	Brighton Village
Roberts Dick	Stubbs Village	...	Stubbs Village
Sam Philip	Reily's Village	...	Reily's Village
Shearman Henry Palmer	Montrose Estate	Leasehold	St. George's Parish, Fountain.
Sheen Abraham	Stubbs Village	Freehold	Stubbs Village
Smith Edward Lisle	Calliaqua	Leasehold	Calliaqua—Parsonage
Thomas Quaco	Victoria Village	Freehold	Victoria Village
Turner Alexander	Stubbs Village	...	Stubbs Village
Theobalds James Alexander	Calliaqua	...	Calliaqua
Tuckett Wallace	...	Leasehold	Calliaqua—Glebe Land
Williams McKee	Harmony Hall	Freehold	Harmony Hall Village
Wilks Pompey	Stubbs Village	...	Stubbs Village
Williams Rodney	Mesopotamia	...	Mesopotamia
Wilson Samuel	Carapan Estate	...	Brighton Village
Wilks William	Stubbs Village	...	Stubbs Village

ELECTORAL DISTRICT No. 4.

Christian and Surname.	Place of Abode.	Nature of Qualification.	Place where the property is situate. Name of the property or other description. Name of Tenant &c.
Adams Aberdeen	Chateaubelair	Freehold	Chateaubelair, St. David's Parish
Alexander Alexis	Barrouallie	Freehold house & land	Barrouallie
Barber John	Belleisle	...	...
Boyd Cupid	Barrouallie	Freehold	...
Bulkeley James	...	Freehold House	...
Carney William	Walibou	Freehold	...

Figure 2   Barbados: Electoral register, 1951. (CO 32/124)

LIST OF ELECTORS

PARISH OF ST. THOMAS— DISTRICT XI.—*Continued.*

NO.	NAME	ADDRESS	OCCUPATION
213.	Jemmott, Ercil	Welchman Hall	Domestic Servant
214.	Jemmott, Ethelbert	Welchman Hall	Labourer
215.	Jemmott, Rupert	Welchman Hall	Carpenter
216.	Jemmott, Viola	Welchman Hall	Hawker
217.	Johnson, Doreen	Highland	Labourer
218.	Johnson, Fitz Albert	Welchman Hall	Carpenter
219.	Johnson, Gwendolyn	Welchman Hall	Labourer
220.	Johnson, Iona	Welchman Hall	Labourer
221.	Johnson, Ione	Highland	Housewife
222.	Jones, Betty Eileen Valdemanr	Canefield Plantation	Housewife
223.	Jones, Kenneth De Lisle	Canefield Plantation	Planter
224.	Jones, Violet	Canefield	Labourer
225.	Jordan, Gwendolyn Verona	Welchman Hall	Any kind of work
226.	Jordan, Whitstandley Glendover	Welchman Hall	Mason
227.	King, Joseph E.	Welchman Hall	Labourer
228.	King, Louise	Porey Spring	Hawker
229.	King, Mary Ann	Welchman Hall	Labourer
230.	Knight, Marie	Highland	Labourer
231.	Knight, Myrtle	Canefield	Labourer
232.	Lawrence, Marguerita	Welchman Hall	Housewife (Widow)
233.	Leacock, Albertha	Welchman Hall	Labourer
234.	Leacock, Elsaline	Porey Spring	Seamstress
235.	Leacock, Gladstone	Welchman Hall	Nil
236.	Leacock, Lilian	Fortress	Labourer
237.	Legall, Millicent	Welchman Hall	Domestic Servant
238.	Leslie, James	Welchman Hall	Labourer
239.	Leslie, Samuel	Dunscombe	Factory Labourer
240.	Leslie, Violet	Dunscombe	Housewife
241.	Lewis, Dora	Canefield	Labourer
242.	Lewis, Courtenay	Highland	Labourer
243.	Lewis, Joseph	Canefield	Labourer
244.	Licorish, Naomi	Welchman Hall	Labourer
245.	Linton, Cloris	Porey Spring	Labourer
246.	Linton, James	Porey Spring	Tailor
247.	Lovell, Lambert	Porey Spring	Labourer
248.	Luke, Oliver	Fortress	Cabinet Maker
249.	Lynch, Augusta	Canefield	Labourer
250.	Lynch, David Agustus	Canefield	Labourer
251.	Mahon, Helen Brequette	Lion Castle	Housewife (Widow)
252.	Mahon, Julian Aubrey	Lion Castle	Planter
253.	Mahon, Mollie Louise	Lion Castle	Housewife
254.	Marshall, Beryl	Welchman Hall	Housewife
255.	Marshall, Cathalene	Welchman Hall	Domestic Servant
256.	Marshall, Westerman	Welchman Hall	Carpenter
257.	Maynard, Anna	Porey Spring	Seamstress
258.	Maynard, Clement Palmy	Porey Spring	Postman
259.	Maynard, Cynthia	Porey Spring	Labourer
260.	Maynard, Eleazor	Canefield	Labourer
261.	Maynard, FitzGerald	Porey Spring	Engineer
262.	Maynard, Ianthe	Welchman Hall	Domestic Servant
263.	Maynard, Lawriston	Porey Spring	Chauffeur
264.	Maynard, Loleta	Porey Spring	Seamstress
265.	Maynard, Maude	Welchman Hall	Labourer
266.	Maynard, Ordine	Welchman Hall	Hawker
267.	Maynard, Osbert	Porey Spring	Tailor
268.	Maynard, Samuel	Porey Spring	Carpenter
269.	Maynard, Tabitha	Canefield	Hawker
270.	McKenzy, Beresford	Dunscombe	Labourer
271.	McKenzy, Lilian	Dunscombe	Labourer
272.	Morris, Maria	Welchman Hall	Nil
273.	Murray, Cecil	Welchman Hall	Labourer
274.	Murray, Genneatha	Canefield	Labourer
275.	Murray, Samuel	Canefield	Labourer
276.	Neblett, Algo	Canefield	Labourer
277.	Neblett, Danverse	Welchman Hall	Mason
278.	Neblett, Octiva	Welchman Hall	Housewife
279.	Nicholls, Arhodah	Porey Spring	Domestic Servant
280.	Nicholls, Carlotta	Highland	Labourer
281.	Nicholls, Cuthbert	Welchman Hall	Tailor
282.	Nicholls, Doreen	Welchman Hall	Seamstress
283.	Nicholls, Lavira	Canefield	Labourer
284.	Niles, Alonza	Welchman Hall	Labourer

Figure 3   St Vincent: list of voters, 1868. (CO 264/9)

95

SUPPLEMENT TO THE GOVERNMENT GAZETTE, of THURSDAY, June 9.

NAMES.	RESIDENCE.	Under Income Tax.	Under Troops Tax.	NAMES.	RESIDENCE.	Under Income Tax.	Under Troops Tax.
John Edward	Belleisle		2 6	Lawrent Thomas	Morne Ronde		3 6
John Moses	Banaye		1 6	Lawrent Antoine	,,		1
John Martin	Chateaubellair	5	8 6	Lawrent John	,,		3 6
John Couma	Coull's	5	3 6	Leach Geo. Wm.	Barrouallie		6
John Joseph	Wallibou		3 6	Leader Agnes	Richmond		3
John Charlotte	Coull's		6	Ledger Margaret	Nicholas-Ledger		5
John Jane	Palmiste		3 6	Leggat Adolphus	Barrouallie		1
John Margaret	Barrouallie		3	Lett Ed. Scott	Lafargue		6
John Alexander	Craigieburn		3 6	Llewellyn Smart	Barrouallie		11
John Alexander	Sandy Bay		6	Llewellyn Eliza	Layou		3
John James	Coull's		8	Lewis Wm.	Barrouallie		16 6
Johnson Thomas	Barrouallie	2 15	3 15 3	Lewis John Pierre	,,		4
Johnson Samuel	Chateaubellair		8	Lewis Noel	,,		3 6
Johnson Mary	Wallibou		6	Lewis Peter	Hermitage		6
Johnson Joseph	,,		4	Lewis John Paul	Richmond		3
Johnson Ann	Hillsboro		4	Lewis Andrew	Wallibou		6
Jones Betsey	Coull's		6	Lewis John	,,		3 6
Joseph Stephen	Evergreen		6	Lewis James	Evergreen		2 6
Joseph Alexander	Palmiste		6	Lewis Andrew	Hillsboro		2
Joseph Mercy	Wallibou		3	Lewis Sophia			3
Joseph George	Barrouallie		4	Lewis Wm.	Wallbou		3 6
Joseph Wm.	Richmond Vale		6	Lewis Jane			1
Joshua Thomas	Wallilabo	5	3	Lewis Diana	Layou		3
Joshua Alexander	Wallibou		6	Lewis James	,,		10 6
Joshua Joseph	Richmond		3 6	Lewis Edward	,,		3
Josiah Joseph	Barrouallie		5 6	Lewis Franky	Coull's		3
Jostin Abraham	Richmond Vale		5	Liscott Frank	Wallibou		3 6
Jouette Wm.	Morne Ronde		3 6	Liverpool John	Richmond Vale		4 6
				Liverpool Israel	Grog River		1
Kairns Robert	Spring		3	Liverpool Sophia	Barrouallie		3 6
Keane Mary	Layou		3	London John	,,		3 6
Keane Mary Ann	,,		10 6	London Thomas	Wallibou		3 6
Keane Ann	,,		3	Longford Moses	Barrouallie		3
Keane Wm.	,,		3	Lord James	L'Ance Mahaut		1
Keane Adelaide	Barrouallie		8	Louis Joseph	Morne Ronde		3 6
Kearton Adelaide	,,		8	Lewis Thomas	,,		3 6
Kearton Bacchus	,,	5	7	Lynch Rebecca	Coull's		4 6
Kearton Douglas	,,	5	1	Lyndsay Job	Barrouallie		3
Kennedy Robert	Morne Ronde	10	1 7				
Kennedy George	Barrouallie		3	Macalister Wm.	Grog river		3
Kirby Allan			3	Macdonald Duncan	Wallilabo	3 5	1 15
Kirby Alvin	L'Ance Mahaut		3	Mack Manoel	Hillsboro		3 6
Kirby Peter	Coull's		5 6	Mack Manny	Craigieburn		4
Kirby James	,,		3 6	MacMahon Thomas	Coull's		3 6
Knight Samuel Enos	Chateaubellair	1 10	1	Mandeville James N.	Barrouallie	10	18 6
Knight Henry	Coulls		5	Mars Telemaque	Lamee's		6
Knight Dolly	,,		4	Mars Edward	Kearton's		6
				Marques Manuel	Belleisle		6
Labbé Alexander	Dyer's Bay		6	Marshal Pierre	Wallibou		3 6
Laborell John	Hillsboro		4 6	Marshal James	,,		6
Lane John	Barrouallie		3	Martin Samuel	Barrouallie		6
Lane Richard	,,		8 6	Martin Orlando	Coull's		3 6
Lane Samuel	,,		6	Martin John	Palmiste		4
Lavington Polly	,,		3 6	Martin John	Sandy Bay		6
Lawrence Francois	Richmond		6	Martin Charles	Barrouallie		3
Lawrence John J.	Layou		4 6	Martin Elizabeth	,,		11
Lawrence Abraham	Chateaubellair		8 6	Martin Francis	Chateaubellair		3

Figure 4   St Vincent: tax return, 1870. (CO 264/9)

11

JURY LIST 1892.

THE following lists of persons qualified and liable to serve as Jurors during the year 1892, is published in accordance with the provisions of "The Jury Ordinance. 1879". Any objections thereto, and any claims for admission or exemption will be heard and determined by the Magistrate of the District to which the person objected to as a Juror, or the person claiming to be admitted or exempted as a Juror, resides, at the first meeting of the Magistrate's Court after the expiration of seven days from the date of this notice.

C. FALCONER ANTON,
Registrar of the Supreme Court.

REGISTRAR'S OFFICE,   }
31st December, 1891. }

Name	Abode.	Calling.	Qualification.
Abraham, Jones	St. Andrew	Planter	Income of not less than £100 ℗ annum.
Aird, David	Parish St. George	Shopkeeper	ditto
Alexander, Edward	Town St. George	ditto	ditto
Alexander, C. A.	St. Andrew	Planter	Owner of real property, value £200.
Alexander, Thomas S.	St. Patrick	Tailor	Income of not less than £100 ℗ annum.
Alexander, Francois	ditto	ditto	ditto
Alexander, Junior Douglas	ditto	Planter	ditto
Alexander, Hall	ditto	ditto	ditto
Alexis, Augustine Nelson	ditto	ditto	ditto
Alexis, Louis	ditto	ditto	Owner of real property, value £200.
Alleyne, S. M.	ditto	Shopkeeper	Income of not less than £100 ℗ annum.
Alleyne, John	ditto	Blacksmith	ditto
Aquart, Peter	St. John	Planter	Owner of real property, value £200.
Attz, A. J. A. A.	Parish St. George	ditto	ditto
Bain, Alexander	St Patrick	ditto	Income not less than £100 ℗ annum.
Bain, Edwin Donald	St. Andrew	Accountant	ditto
Baptiste, Alexander John	Town St. George	Shopkeeper	ditto
Batt, John	St. Andrew	Accountant	ditto
Bayne, Wm. F.	St. John	Planter	ditto
Begg, Samuel	St. David	ditto	Owner of real property, value £200.
Belfon, Peter	St. Patrick	ditto	Income of not less than £100 ℗ annum.
Bell, James	ditto	ditto	Owner of real property, value £200.
Belton, Robert Andrew	St. John	Merchant	ditto
Bennett, Charles	ditto	Planter	ditto
Berkeley, John H. Astley	St. Andrew	ditto	ditto
Bertrand, John	ditto	Merchant	ditto
Bertrand, Clement	ditto	ditto	ditto
Bertrand, Francis S.	ditto	ditto	ditto
Bertrand, James M.	ditto	ditto	Income of not less than £100 ℗ annum.
Best, Arthur James	ditto	Planter	Owner of real property, value £200.
Branch, William D.	ditto	ditto	ditto
Browne, Peter	St. Andrew	ditto	Income of not less than £100 ℗ annum.
Browne, Robert Jos.	St. David	ditto	ditto
Browne, Seton	St. Andrew	ditto	ditto
Campbell, Philip J.	Town St. George	ditto	Owner of real property, value £200.
Cape, Joseph	St. Andrew	Shopkeeper	Income of not less than £100 ℗ annum.
Carberry, D. A.	St. Mark's	Clerk	ditto
Carney, Wm. A.	St. Patrick	Planter	Owner real property, value £200.
Canning, Charles	ditto	ditto	ditto
Charles, Joseph	Town St. George	Clerk	ditto
Clyne, Fras. Cornelius H.	St. John	Planter	ditto
Cross, Isaac A.	St. Patrick's	ditto	Income of not less than £100 ℗ annum.
Cruickshank, F. W. R.	Town St. George	Clerk	Owner real of property, value £200.
Copland, John	St. Patrick	Merchant	ditto
Copland, William	St. Mark	Planter	Income of not less than £200 ℗ annum.
Copland, David	ditto	ditto	ditto
Cornewall, Wilson J.	St. Patrick	Carpenter	Owner of real property, value £200.
Cox, Edward Byron	Town St. George	Blacksmith	Income of not less than £100 ℗ annum.
Creed, James	ditto	Tailor	ditto
Crick, Richd. Aug.	ditto	Merchant	ditto
Cruickshank, William	Parish St. George	Planter	Owner of real property, value £200.
Dabreo, John	Town St. George	Clerk	Income of not less than £100 ℗ annum.

Figure 5   Grenada: jury list, 1892. (CO 105/9)

POLICE NOTICES.

WANTED by the Police, JAMES WILLIAM *alias* MOTION, for theft of Nutmegs.
DESCRIPTION:—

Age	23 years,
Colour	Black,
Height	5ft. 7 inches,
Build	Slender,
Teeth	Upper front very much decayed,
Occupation	Labourer,
Native of	Grenada,

Leans to the right when walking.

R. T. WRIGHT,
Chief of Police,

CHIEF OF POLICE OFFICE,
17th May, 1892.

DESCRIPTION of JAKE MUNRO for whom a warrant is issued—

Height	5ft. 2 inches,
Age	14 years,
Face	Small and thin,
Eyes	Black,
Hair	Black and Woolly,
Colour	Black,
Teeth	Lost 3 in front,
Build	Slight.

R. T. WRIGHT.
Chief of Police.

CHIEF OF POLICE OFFICE,
ST. GEORGE'S, 4 May, 1892.

GOVERNMENT GAZETTE, 17 FEBRUARY, 1892.—(No. 10.)   65

Three hundred acres or thereabouts which said plantation is delineated in a plan or diagram thereof drawn in the margin of a Conveyance bearing date the 16th day of July 1878 and made by the Commissioners for Sale of Incumbered Estates in the West Indies to ALEXANDER WARD.

Conditions of Sale may be seen at this Office and also at the Chambers of the Hon'ble W. S. COMISSIONG from and after the 10th day of March next.

5th February, 1892.

Suit No. 102 of 1891.

Between WILLIAM DAVID MARTIN and PETER JOHNSON DEAN trading together under the style or firm of Martin Dean and Company, *Plaintiffs.*
and
ALEXANDER FRASER and ANN BRONNLEE his wife. *Defendants.*

PURSUANT to an order of this Honorable Court made in this Cause on the 8th day of December 1891 there will be offered for sale at the Court House in the Town of St. George on *Friday the 26th day of February next* at 3 o'clock in the afternoon. All that LOT PIECE or PARCEL of LAND called Annsfield formerly part of Annandale Estate situate in the parish of St. George in the Island of Grenada containing by admeasurement one Rood English Statute Measure and abutted and bounded on the North West and South by lands of Joseph John Pierre and on the East by a Public Road or howsoever otherwise the same may be abutted and bounded together with the messuages and buildings thereon.

23rd January 1892.

Suit No. 72 of 1891.

COURT OF ESCHEAT.

THE sitting of this Court, advertised to be held on the 8th instant, is hereby postponed to *Monday the 22nd instant.*

W. S. COMISSIONG,
Escheator General.

CHAMBERS,
2nd February, 1892.

TO ALL WHOM IT MAY CONCERN.

COURT OF ESCHEAT.

A sitting of this Court will be held at the Court House in the town of St. George, on *Monday the 8th day of February next,* at 12 o'clock noon, for the purpose of trying the right of the Crown to the undermentioned lands and tenements.

1. A LOT OF LAND part of Old St. Cyr Estate situate in the parish of Saint Andrew containing about three acres, late the property of John Young who died intestate and without heirs.
2. A LOT OF LAND part of Old St. Cyr Estate aforesaid, containing about two acres late the property of John Louis Berkeley who died intestate and without heirs.
3. A LOT OF LAND with a messuage thereon situate in Grenville Street in the town of Saint George late the property of Mary Rennie Hanket who died intestate and without heirs.
4. A LOT OF LAND part of Paraclete Estate situate in the parish of Saint Andrew contain-

Figure 6   a) Grenada: police notice describing 2 felons. (CO 105/9)
b) Grenada: sales of land in Court of Escheat. (CO 105/9)

Figure 7   Barbados: *The Liberal* newspaper showing lists of occupiers, etc.
(CO 33/12, f 123)

For family and local historians the gazettes can provide a wealth of information. Examples include birth, marriage, and death notices, occasionally including obituaries of notable persons; notices of proceedings and sales in the courts of chancery and petty sessions; lists of people applying for liquor, dog, and gun licences; lists of jurors, druggists (chemists), constables, voters, solicitors, nurses, medical practitioners, and militia; notices of sales of land; public appointments, leave of absence and resumption of duty; notices relating to cases of intestacy, guardianship, and wills; notices on applications for naturalization; inquests into shipwrecks; ships entering and clearing port, sometimes with the names of first class passengers; people paid parish relief; and tax lists.

3.6 Miscellanea

Miscellanea classes contain primarily Blue Books of Statistics, but for some colonies they also contain newspapers and naval officers' returns.

3.6.1 Blue Books of Statistics: annual books which begin about 1820 and continue until the mid-1940s. They contain statistical information about the colony, such as population, education, religion, and economy. They also include names of public employees and pensioners.

3.6.2 Naval office returns: customs returns taken at colonial ports. They record the names of incoming and outgoing vessels, the master, the owner, port of registry, tonnage, number of crew, type of goods, and the previous and next port.

3.6.3 Newspapers: an incomplete series of newspapers received by the Colonial Office during the 1830s to 1850s. They are similar to government gazettes. The British Library Newspaper Library, Colindale, London NW9 5HE, contains collections of colonial newspapers.

3.7 Registers of Correspondence

Between 1703 and 1759 manuscript calendars of the correspondence of the Board of Trade are found in the General Registers (CO 326/1-51). From 1759 to 1782 an annual calendar was produced (CO 326/52-74). From 1822 to

1849 all incoming correspondence was entered in a series of registers (CO 326/85-358) arranged by groups of colonies.

In 1849 the Colonial Office introduced a system of registration whereby every incoming letter was allocated a number in the Daily Register (CO 382), which started with '1' each year. Details of the letter were then entered in a register for the colony. There is a class of these registers of correspondence, which ran until 1951, for each colony. Until 1926 the following details were noted in columns: date of registration; registered number (taken from the daily register); name of the correspondent; date of letter; despatch number; subject of letter and a brief précis; related correspondence; action taken; and remarks. The cross-references contained in the registers are abbreviated and usually refer to other correspondence recorded in the same register. For example, 'Gov' refers to Governor's despatches, 'MO' to Miscellaneous Offices, and 'C' to individuals beginning with 'C'. A table of abbreviations is in *Sources for Colonial Studies in the Public Record Office, I*, pp 399-400. Other information may be stamped into the register, such as 'Destroyed under statute', where the letter has been destroyed; 'Printed for Parliament', with the date, these can be found in the House of Commons Sessional Papers; 'Printed for the Colonial Office', with a colony and number noted, these are Colonial Office Confidential Print; and 'Secret', these papers are often filed in CO 537. The letter was then given a minute sheet onto which were written similar details as in the register, and which was used by Colonial Office officials to note comments. Draft replies may be attached to the letter.

Until 1926 the registers are arranged firstly by the governor's despatches; then by letters from British government departments; and then by letters from individuals. Increasingly from 1868 the 'Individuals' section may be used as an index to individuals and subjects mentioned in the correspondence. At the end of each register there is often a list of printed material received from the colony, such as acts, blue books, and sessional papers. It is important to note that the registers are arranged by the date of registration but the original correspondence is filed by the date of the letter.

In 1926 a series of annual subject files was introduced, whereby each colony was allocated a block of file numbers. The registers continue in the same classes as before but they are arranged in file number order. There is usually a key to the files in the front of each volume. The registers give a brief description of each letter filed under the subject, the date and name of sender, and the action taken. If the letter was destroyed or printed this will also be recorded.

3.8 Registers of Out-letters

There is a class of registers of out-letters for each colony. They continue from the entry books (section 3.2), starting in 1872 and running until 1926. These are compiled in the date order of the outgoing correspondence from the Colonial Office. The registers are arranged firstly by governor, then government department, and finally the individual, with whom the Colonial Office was corresponding. They record the name of recipient, date of despatch, number of despatch, a brief description, and the registered number of the letter to which it was the reply. Unlike the entry books, these give only a précis of each outgoing letter. If a draft copy survives it will be in the appropriate original correspondence class.

Further reading:

PRO Records Information Leaflets

23 - *Records of the American and West Indian Colonies before 1782.*

86 - *Records of the Colonial and Dominions Offices from 1782.*

Andrews, Charles M, *Guide to the Materials for American History to 1783 in the Public Record Office of Great Britain*, 2 vols (Washington, Carnegie Institution of Washington, 1912 and 1914).

Bell, Herbert C and Parker, David W, *Guide to British West Indian Archive Materials in London and in the Islands for the History of the United States* (Washington, Carnegie Institution of Washington, 1926).

Calendar of State Papers, Colonial, America and West Indies, 1574-1739, 40 vols (London, HMSO, 1860-1993).

Journals of the Board of Trade and Plantations, 1704-1782, 14 vols (London: HMSO, 1920-1938).

Anne Thurston, *Sources for Colonial Studies in the Public Record Office, I: Records of the Colonial Office, Dominions Office, Commonwealth Relations Office and Commonwealth Office* (London, HMSO, 1995)

Ragatz, Lowell Joseph, *A Guide to the Official Correspondence of the Governors of the British West India Colonies with the Secretary of State, 1763-1833* (London, The Bryan Edwards Press, 1923).

Walne, Peter, ed, *A Guide to Manuscript Sources for the History of Latin America and the Caribbean in the British Isles* (Oxford University Press, 1973).

Chapter 4: How People Got to the West Indies

4.1 Passenger Lists

Very few passenger lists survive in the PRO before 1890. The British government did not register people emigrating from these shores, and until the First World War it was not necessary for emigrants to have passports.

Licences to pass beyond the seas (E 157) include registers of passengers going to America and the West Indies between 1634 and 1639, and in 1677. Port Books (E 190) are customs accounts and often include names of passengers. The Privy Council registers (PC 2) contain many petitions and letters of people emigrating to, or already settled in, the colonies. These and other Privy Council papers relating to the colonies, 1613-1783, are described in *Acts of the Privy Council, Colonial Series.* Passenger lists in the PRO prior to 1890 do not contain much information on emigrants apart from their names, where they sailed from, and the intended destination of the ship. Between 1773 and 1776 a register (T 47/9-12) was made of emigrants going from England, Wales and Scotland to the Americas. The information given is name, age, occupation, reason for leaving the country, last place of residence, date of departure, and destination. A card index is available in the Reference Room at Kew. Many early passenger lists are to be found among the records of the Colonial Office. Many of these sources have been published and are included in the bibliography.

Colonial newspapers and government gazettes occasionally give the names of first class passengers in the shipping intelligence sections.

From 1890, the Board of Trade kept passenger lists of people leaving from British ports to places outside Europe and the Mediterranean. These passenger lists (BT 27) are arranged by date, by port of departure and by ship. Information given in the lists includes the name, age and occupation of each passenger, and often the place of residence in Britain. These records run until 1960.

> **Further reading:**
> PRO Records Information Leaflets
> 71 - *Emigrants*
> *Tracing Your Ancestors*, section 14

Acts of the Privy Council, Colonial Series, 1613-1783, 6 volumes (London, 1908-1912).

Coldham, Peter Wilson, *The Complete Book of Emigrants*, 4 vols, 1607-1776 (Baltimore, Genealogical Publishing Co, Inc, 1987-1993).

Coldham, Peter Wilson, *Emigrants from England to the American Colonies* (Baltimore, Genealogical Publishing Co, Inc, 1983).

Dobson, David, *Directory of Scottish Settlers in North America, 1625-1825*, 6 vols (Baltimore, Genealogical Publishing Co, Inc, 1984-1986).

Filby, P W, and Meyer, M K, *Passenger and Immigration Lists Index*, 3 vols (Detroit, Gale Research Company, 1981). (This is a bibliographic guide to 500,000 names taken from published passenger lists to America in the 17th to 19th centuries. From 1982 there are annual supplements of some 150,000 names each.)

Hotten, John Camden, *The Original Lists of Persons of Quality...and Others Who Went from Great Britain to the American Plantations 1600-1700* (Baltimore, Genealogical Publishing Co, Inc, 1980).

4.2 Indentured Servants

Once the West Indies were settled there was a high demand for cheap labour. This was met initially by indentured servants from Britain, and then later by African slave labour. Indentured servants were shipped to the colonies by agents who arranged a transport fee through colonial merchants. They were transported free but had to serve a period of seven to ten years. After their period of servitude they were supposed to be allotted ten acres of land. In the more densely populated islands, such as Barbados, this did not always occur. The PRO does not hold lists of indentured servants, and where they survive they are to be found in local record offices, especially for London, Liverpool and Bristol where the agents resided.

Further reading

Clark, Peter, and Souden, David, *Migration and Society in Early Modern England* (London, Hutchinson, 1987)

Coldham, Peter Wilson, *The Bristol Registers of Servants Sent to Foreign Plantations, 1654-1686* (Baltimore, Genealogical Publishing Co, Inc, 1988).

Kaminkow, Jack and Marion, *A List of Emigrants from England to America, 1718-1759* (Baltimore, Magna Charta Book Co, 1964).

4.3 Transportation

From 1615, until the loss of the mainland American colonies in 1783, many thousands of people were sentenced to transportation, or had a death sentence commuted to transportation, and were shipped to the American colonies. Many of these, especially in the early- to mid-1600s, were transported to the West Indies, but most records do not state the final destination. Transportation was for ten years as most of the colonies forbade longer sentences. Merchants arranged for shipment of transportees and, if on arrival in the colonies they were not already allocated an estate to work on, they were put up for auction.

State Papers, Domestic (SP classes) contain correspondence, petitions, and lists of reprieved persons concerning transportation. Up to 1704 these are calendared in the *Calendars of State Papers, Domestic*. Lists of persons to be transported occur in the Patent Rolls (C 66), the Treasury Papers (T 1, 1747-1772) and the Treasury Money Books (T 53, 1716-1744). Until 1745 the Treasury papers are described in the *Calendars of Treasury Books and Papers*. Trials and verdicts of cases tried by the assize circuits are to be found among the various ASSI classes. Governors' despatches and colonial entry books also describe cases and policy concerning transportation. Other records such as Quarter Sessions, transportation bonds and landing certificates are to be found in local record offices.

From 1783 other destinations were sought and Australia became Britain's next penal colony.

Further reading
PRO Records Information Leaflets

26 - *Assizes records*

Tracing Your Ancestors, section 40

Calendar of State Papers, Colonial, America and West Indies, 1574-1738, 39 vols (HMSO, 1860-1970).

Calendar of Treasury Papers, 1557-1728, 6 vols (HMSO, 1868-1889).

Calendar of Treasury Books, 1660-1718, 32 vols (HMSO, 1904-1962).

Calendar of Treasury Books and Papers, 1729-1745, 5 vols (HMSO, 1898-1903).

Coldham, Peter Wilson, *Bonded Passengers to America*, 3 vols (Baltimore, Genealogical Publishing Co, Inc, 1983).

Coldham, Peter Wilson, *The Complete Book of Emigrants in Bondage, 1614-1775* (Baltimore, Genealogical Publishing Co, Inc, 1988).

Coldham, Peter Wilson, *Emigrants in Chains* (Baltimore, Genealogical Publishing Co, Inc, 1992).

Oldham, Wilfred, *Britain's Convicts to the Colonies* (Sydney, Library of Australian History, 1990).

4.4 Slave Trade

Slavery became established in the British colonies from the 1640s when sugar cane was introduced by Dutch merchants from Brazil. Sugar farming created a monoculture which was physically demanding and required large numbers of labourers. Africans were used to tropical climates, diseases, and food, and were considered more suitable than white indentured labourers. It has been estimated that some 1.6 million slaves were transported to the British West Indies between 1640 and 1808.

The slave trade was essentially a triangular trade where merchants traded British goods for slaves from factories and forts on the West Coast of Africa. These slaves were then traded for goods such as sugar, rum, and molasses, in the West Indies. Prior to 1698 the British slave trade was monopolized by various African companies, which survived until 1821 when the government bought the Royal African Company and its West African forts and settlements. The records of the African companies are in T 70. These records include details of payment for shipments of slaves, names of employees of the African companies, and of their agents in Africa and the West Indies, and general correspondence.

Most of the records relating to the slave trade to be found in the PRO consist of petitions from merchants, statistics of imported slaves, and navy office returns. These are to be found among the records of the Colonial Office. Details of the crews of slaving vessels can be found in the ships' musters in BT 98, although very few survive before 1800.

Until 1808 there are no lists of slaves transported from Africa. Any that occur after that date arise because slave ships had been seized for illegally transporting slaves. The slaves then became forfeited to the crown. These are discussed later under Liberated Africans (section 4.5) and slave registration (section 8.1).

Further reading:

Curtin, Philip D, *The Atlantic Slave Trade. A Census* (University of Wisconsin Press, 1969).

Donnan, Elizabeth, *Documents Illustrative of the History of the Slave Trade to America*, 4 vols (Washington, Carnegie Institution, 1930-1935).

Walvin, James, *Black Ivory. A History of British Slave Trade* (London, Harper Collins Publishers, 1992).

4.5 Liberated Africans

The slave trade was abolished on 1 May 1807 (Abolition of the Slave Trade Act 1807), although vessels which sailed before that date could under certain circumstances trade until 1 March 1808. Any vessels seized under the 1807 act and subsequent acts for illegally carrying slaves were condemned, the master was fined, and the slaves became forfeited to the crown. This meant that they became government slaves, and many were enlisted into the Royal Navy or the army, especially the West India regiments and the Royal African Corps.

The trials of illegal slavers were held at vice-admiralty courts in Africa, the West Indies, Havana and Rio de Janeiro. Under various treaties with slave trading powers such as the Netherlands, Portugal, Spain and Brazil, ships of these and other nations could be sentenced at Mixed Commission Courts. Proceedings, and other papers relating to illegal slave trading are to be found mainly among the records of the Foreign Office, especially those of the Slave Trade Department (FO 84) and the Mixed Commission Courts. The primary court was held at Sierra Leone (FO 315, 1819-1868). The other courts were at Cape Town (FO 312, 1843-1870); Havana (FO 313, 1819-1869); Jamaica (FO 314, 1843-1851); Rio de Janeiro (FO 129/3-13, 15, 1819-1861, and FO 131/1-11, 1820-1885). The records include registers of slaves liberated, crew lists and log books of captured ships, and correspondence with the Admiralty and Foreign Office. Other records can be found in the papers of the Admiralty (ADM 1), the Slave Trade Adviser of the High Court of Admiralty (HCA 37, Colonial customs returns (CUST 34), Colonial Office original correspondence classes, and the Treasury (T 1).

In 1808 Sierra Leone became the centre for British suppression of the slave trade on the West Coast of Africa with the creation of vice-admiralty courts and Mixed Commission Courts to deal with cases of illegal slave trading. Many Liberated Africans settled in Sierra Leone. In the 1840s many freed slaves emigrated to Jamaica and other West Indian islands. Correspondence concerning this emigration, petitions, and some passenger lists are to be found in CO 267.

4.6 East Indians

When slavery was abolished the newly freed slaves had to serve a period of four years for their former masters. This was known as apprenticeship. When apprenticeship ended in 1838 in colonies with available land such as Trinidad, St Vincent and British Guiana, the freed slaves left their owners to establish their own farmsteads. As a result, many islands suffered severe labour shortages and petitioned the crown to help relieve this problem. Chinese labour was already being in used in Trinidad from 1806, and later migrant workers from other West Indian islands, Liberated Africans, and Portuguese from Madeira and the Azores were encouraged.

The most successful group of migrants was the East Indians; often referred to in the records as 'coolies'. Policy papers concerning their recruitment are to be found among appropriate geographical correspondence classes, CO 323 and CO 318. CO 318 contains specific sections devoted to Indian labour for the period 1843-1873 These are continued in CO 323, and later in the Immigration Department records in CO 571, 1913-1920.

From the 1870s the records of the Land Board and Emigration Department, CO 384-CO 386, registers in CO 428, are concerned with emigration to the West Indies. These related mainly to Chinese and Indian emigration. CO 384 and CO 385 include surgeons' reports for emigrant ships which sometimes detail births and deaths. Other papers record ships commissioned to sail from Madras and Calcutta with the numbers of Indians on board. Lists of these emigrants may be found in the colonial correspondence and government gazettes.

The Indian sub-continent was administered by the East India Company, and from 1858 by the India Office. The records of these organizations are held by

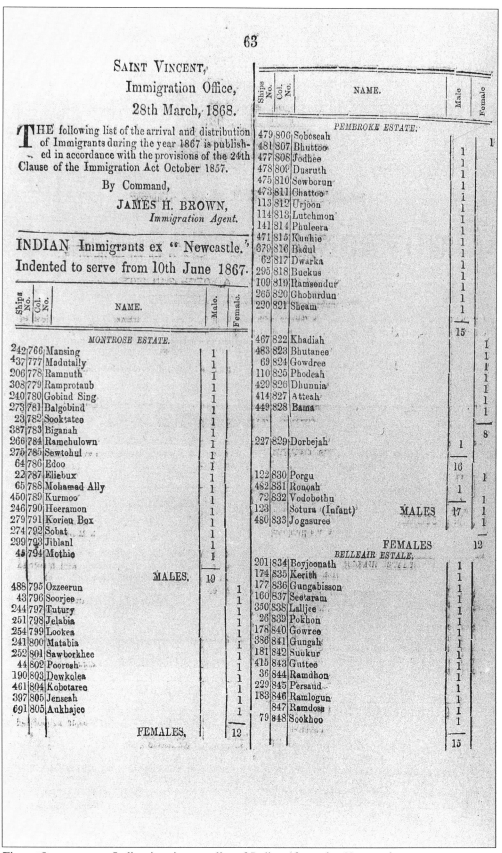

63

SAINT VINCENT,

Immigration Office,

28th March, 1868.

THE following list of the arrival and distribution of Immigrants during the year 1867 is published in accordance with the provisions of the 24th Clause of the Immigration Act October 1857.

By Command,

JAMES H. BROWN,
Immigration Agent.

INDIAN Immigrants ex " Newcastle."
Indented to serve from 10th June 1867.

Ships No.	Col. No.	NAME.	Male.	Female.
		MONTROSE ESTATE.		
242	766	Mansing	1	
437	777	Madutally	1	
206	778	Ramnuth	1	
308	779	Ramprotaub	1	
240	780	Gobind Sing	1	
273	781	Balgobind	1	
23	782	Sooktatee	1	
387	783	Biganah	1	
266	784	Ramchulown	1	
275	785	Sewtohul	1	
64	786	Edoo	1	
22	787	Eliebux	1	
65	788	Mohamad Ally	1	
450	789	Kurmoo	1	
246	790	Heeramon	1	
279	791	Korieu Box	1	
274	792	Sobat	1	
299	793	Jiblanl	1	
45	794	Mothie	1	
		MALES.	19	
488	795	Ozzeerun		1
43	796	Soorjee		1
244	797	Tutury		1
251	798	Jelabia		1
254	799	Lookea		1
241	800	Matabia		1
252	801	Sawborkhee		1
44	802	Poorosh		1
190	803	Dewkolea		1
461	804	Kobotaree		1
397	805	Jenseah		1
691	805	Aukhajee		1
		FEMALES.		12

Ships No.	Col. No.	NAME.	Male	Female
		PEMBROKE ESTATE.		
479	806	Soboseah		1
481	807	Bhuttoo	1	
477	808	Jodhee	1	
478	809	Dusruth	1	
475	810	Sewborun	1	
473	811	Ghattoo	1	
113	812	Urjoon	1	
114	813	Lutchmon	1	
141	814	Phuleera	1	
471	815	Kunhie	1	
679	816	Badul	1	
62	817	Dwarka	1	
295	818	Buckus	1	
109	819	Ramsondur	1	
265	820	Ghoburdun	1	
230	821	Sheam	1	
			15	
467	822	Khadiah		1
483	823	Bhutanee		1
69	824	Gowdree		1
110	825	Phodeah		1
429	826	Dhunnia		1
414	827	Atteah		1
449	828	Bama		1
				8
227	829	Dorbejah	1	
			16	
122	830	Porgu		1
482	831	Ronqah	1	
72	832	Vodobothu		1
123		Sotura (Infant) MALES	17	1
480	833	Jogasuree		1
		FEMALES		12
		BELLEAIR ESTATE.		
201	834	Boyjoonath		1
174	835	Kerith		1
177	836	Gungabisson		1
160	837	Seetaram		1
350	838	Lalljee		1
26	839	Pokhon		1
178	840	Gowree		1
386	841	Gungah		1
181	842	Suukur		1
415	843	Guttee		1
36	844	Ramdhon		1
229	845	Persaud		1
183	846	Ramlogun		1
	847	Ramdoss		1
79	848	Sookhoo		1
				15

Figure 8   Indian immigrants; list of Indians from the *Newcastle*.
(CO 264/9, pp 63-64)

the Oriental and India Office Collections, British Library, 197 Blackfriars Road, London SE1 8NG. The records of the agents who arranged for the transportation of Indians to the West Indies may survive in the National Archives of India, Janpeth, New Delhi 110001, India.

Further reading:

Thomas, Timothy N, *Indians Overseas. A Guide to Source Materials in the India Office Records for the Study of Indian Emigration, 1830-1950* (London: British library, 1985).

Saha, Panchanan, *Emigration of Indian Labour (1834-1900)* (New Delhi, People Publishing House, 1970).

4.7 American Loyalists

During and after the American War of Independence, 1775-1783, many people lost their land and possessions because of their loyalty to the British crown. Many loyalists fled to Britain and Nova Scotia. The 'Book of Negroes' (PRO 30/55/100, no 10427), compiled by British military authorities in 1783, lists black refugees in New York prior to leaving for Nova Scotia. Many are recorded as having been in the West Indies. Many also left for the West Indies, in particular to the Bahamas and Jamaica. Under the Treaty of Peace (1783) and the Treaty of Amity (1794) they were able to claim compensation for their losses. The records of Treasury Commissioners investigating claims, with pension and compensation lists, are in T 50, 1780-1835, T 79, 1777-1841, AO 12, 1776-1831, and AO 13, 1780-1835.

Former slaves of Americans who fought for the British cause were allowed to remain free. Many of these Black Loyalists who escaped to Nova Scotia and England became the initial settlers of Sierra Leone which was established in 1787 by a group of philanthropists as a settlement for freed slaves from Britain and the West Indies. The proceedings and other papers of the Committee for the Relief of Poor Blacks are among the papers in T 1/631-638, 641-647. Four hundred poor blacks together with some English women were transported as the first settlers to Sierra Leone; a list of those at Plymouth, 16 February 1787, is in T 1/643, no 487. The settlement did not survive and in 1791 a group of Black Loyalists from Nova Scotia was encouraged to settle. A list of the blacks of Birch Town, Nova Scotia, who gave their names for Sierra Leone, November 1791, is in CO 217/63, ff 361-366. Their numbers increased with the arrival in 1800 of Jamaican Maroons, who had been expelled from Jamaica for Nova Scotia in 1796.

Further reading:

PRO Records Information Leaflets

34 - *American Land Grants and American Loyalists*

Coldham, Peter Wilson, *American Loyalist Claims* (Washington, National Genealogical Society, 1992).

Walker, James W St G, *The Black Loyalists. The Search for a Promised Land in Nova Scotia and Sierra Leone, 1783-1870* (Longman & Dalhousie University Press, 1976).

Chapter 5: Life Cycle Records

These are the primary sources for a family historian which cover the major events in the lives of individuals: birth, marriage and death. In this section I have included West Indian censuses, and records of wills.

5.1 Records of births, marriages and deaths

5.1.1 Slaves

Slaves were chattel, which meant that they were the personal property of their owner. Most of the events which affected their lives were plantation affairs, and records of births and deaths were events that would be recorded by their owner, if at all. On plantations, slaves had a value according to their occupation, sex and age, and were often listed with livestock. These records are private records and are described in section 6.3 on Plantation records. Other sources for slave birth and death events are church parish registers, where baptisms and burials were recorded. However, in the older colonies, until the late 1700s slaves were actively discouraged from attending church. In Barbados owners were fined, or even expelled, for allowing their slaves to attend church.

The most important records in the PRO concerning slave births and deaths are the slave registers in T 71 (section 8.1) which run from 1812 to 1834. The registration of slaves was carried out approximately every three years and each owner was required to list changes from the last registration. It is possible to estimate the year of birth or death of a slave from the registers.

5.1.2 Free persons

Before civil registration the events of birth, marriage and death were recorded in church registers. They recorded baptisms, rather than births, and burials, rather than deaths. The Church of England was the primary church until the 1800s, and followed the same practices as the Church in Britain. From the early 1800s other churches were established, such as Methodist, Moravian, and Baptist.

The PRO holds very few returns from parish registers (see below), and where they survive they are to be found in the relevant West Indian archive. Some

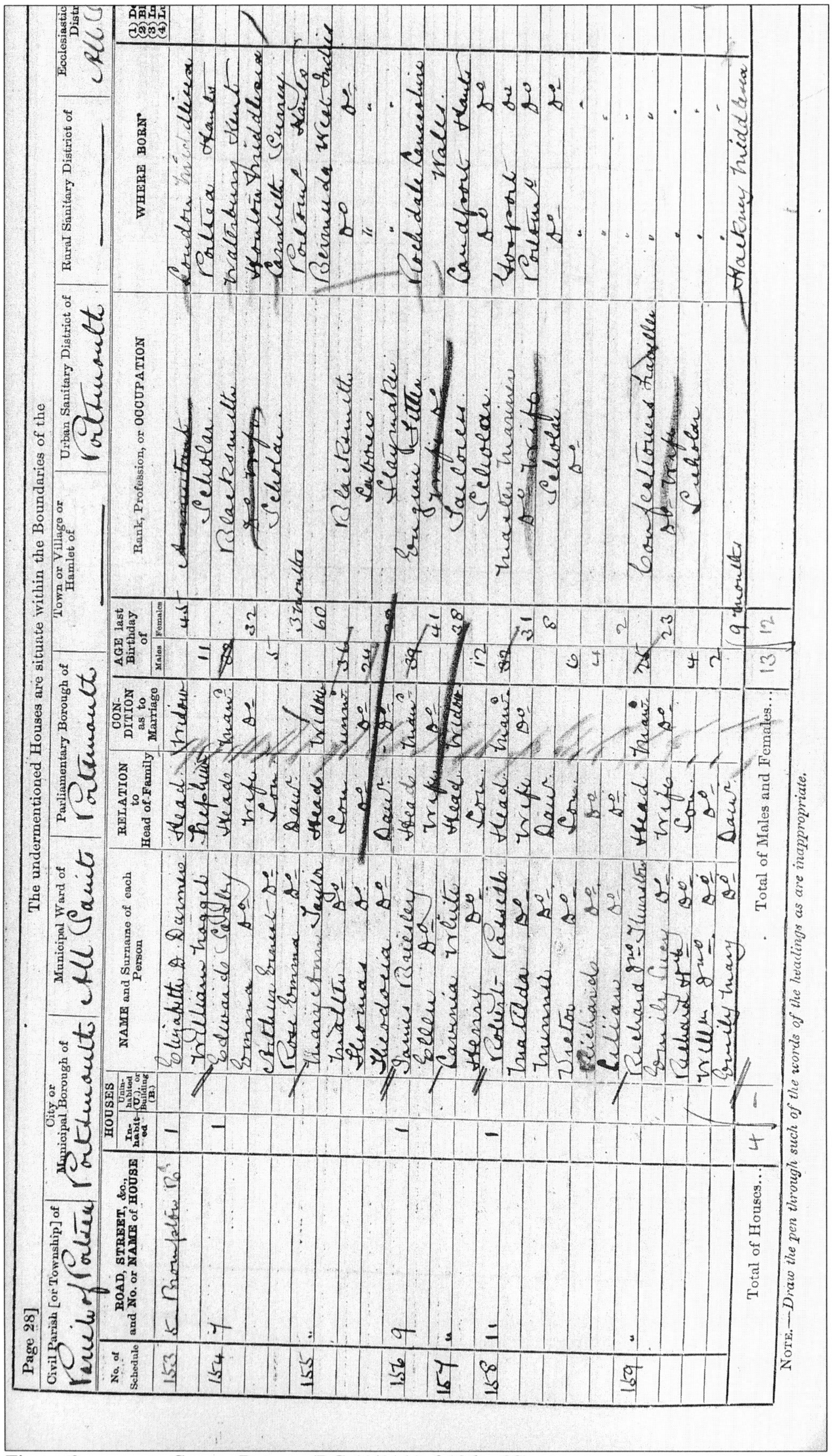

Page 28]

The undermentioned Houses are situate within the Boundaries of the

Civil Parish [or Township] of	City or Municipal Borough of	Municipal Ward of	Parliamentary Borough of	Town or Village or Hamlet of	Urban Sanitary District of	Rural Sanitary District of	Ecclesiastical District
Parish of Portsea	Portsmouth	All Saints	Portsmouth	—	Portsmouth	—	All S[…]

No. of Schedule	ROAD, STREET, &c., and No. or NAME of HOUSE	HOUSES: Inhabited	HOUSES: Uninhabited (U.), or Building (B.)	NAME and Surname of each Person	RELATION to Head of Family	CONDITION as to Marriage	AGE last Birthday of Males	AGE last Birthday of Females	Rank, Profession, or OCCUPATION	WHERE BORN
153	5 Brompton Rd	1		Elizabeth D. Darnes	Head	Widow		45	~~Accountant~~	London Middlesex
				William Haggel	Nephew		11		Scholar	Portsea Hants
154	7	1		Edward C. Cobly?	Head	Mar	32?		Blacksmith	Waterbury Kent
				Emma Do	Wife	Do		32	~~Do Wife~~	Hounslow Middlesex
				Arthur Ernest Do	Son		5		Scholar	Camberwell Surrey
				Rose Emma Do	Daur			3 months		Portsmouth Hants
155	"			Mary Ann Taylor	Head	Widow		60		Bermuda West Indies
				Walter Do	Son	Unm	36		Blacksmith	Do Do
				Thomas Do	Do	Do	24		Labourer	" "
				Theodocia Do	Daur	Do		20?	Staymaker	"
156	9	1		James Brierley	Head	Mar	39		Engine Fitter	Rochdale Lancashire
				Ellen Do	Wife	Do		41	~~Wife Do~~	Wales
157	"			Lavinia White	Head	Widow		38	Tailoress	Landport Hants
				Henry Do	Son		12		Scholar	Do Do
158	11	1		Robert Passells?	Head	Mar	32?		Master Mariner	Gosport Do
				Matilda Do	Wife	Do		31	~~Do Wife~~	Portsmouth Do
				Minnie Do	Daur			8	Scholar	Do Do
				Victor Do	Son		6		Do	" "
				Richards Do	Do		4			" "
				Lillian Do	Do			2		" "
159	"			Richard Jno Thurston	Head	Mar	25		Confectioners Traveller	" "
				Emily Lucy Do	Wife	Do		23	Do Wife	"
				Richard Hy Do	Son		4		Scholar	"
				William Jno Do	Do		2			"
				Emily Mary Do	Daur			9 months		Hackney Middlesex
	Total of Houses...	4	—	Total of Males and Females...			13	12		

NOTE.—*Draw the pen through such of the words of the headings as are inappropriate.*

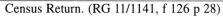

Figure 9 Census Return. (RG 11/1141, f 126 p 28)

West Indian parish registers have been microfilmed by the Church of Latter-Day Saints (Mormons) and can be made available in their family history centres. At the time of writing some Barbadian and Jamaican registers are available at their Hyde Park Family History Centre. The Mormons have also compiled a microfiche index of many millions of baptisms and marriages, for the period about 1550 to 1880. This vast index is called the International Genealogical Index, commonly known as the IGI. They have a programme of identifying all births and marriages and entering them onto the index. The IGI is arranged geographically, and there is a section for the Caribbean. However, the current edition for 1993 covers only Barbados for the British West Indies. The Institute of Genealogical and Heraldic Research, Northgate, Canterbury, Kent CT1 1BA, holds some volumes of Antiguan marriage licences.

Newspapers and colonial gazettes sometimes have notices of births, marriages and deaths, especially of prominent citizens.

Most free people of modest means would have owned at least one slave as a domestic servant. An important source for the period 1817 to 1834 is the slave registers in T 71 which were compiled to establish legally held slaves (section 8.1). They can be used to provide information not only on slaves but also their owners. Changes in ownership are shown in the registers. On the death of an owner slaves were often bequeathed to family members, and on marriage slaves were transferred as property from wife to husband, as a dowry, or a present. Many registers are indexed, while others are arranged alphabetically by plantation, or name of the registered holder.

5.1.3 Colonial Office returns of baptisms, etc

Antigua

1726-1727 CO 152/16
baptisms and burials: St Peter (ff 213-214).

1733-1734 CO 152/21
baptisms and burials: St Paul (ff 123-124, 127-128); St Mary (ff 125-126).

1739-1745 CO 152/25
burials and marriages: St John, 1745 (ff 100-102).

MARRIED.

On Thursday last, at the Cathedral, by the Rev. W. W. JACKSON, WILLIAM PHAROAH, only son of JOHN STRAKER THOMAS, Esq., to SARAH, daughter of JOSEPH COLLYMORE, Esq., Schoolmaster.

This morning, at the Cathedral, by the Rev. H. R. REDWAR, Mr. SAMUEL M. WALROND, to Miss ELIZA HARRUP.

THE LIBERAL, WEDNESDAY, AUGU

DIED.

On Thursday the 17th instant, at 'Rose Garden,' Christ Church, aged 41, JOHN CADDELL BRERETON, Esq., M. D.

At "Mount Gay," St. Lucy's, on Monday night, the 21st instant, HENRY GRANNUM, Esq

On the 21st instant, in Bay-street, Mrs. SARAH TYSON ROGERS, aged 76 years, mother of Mr. WILLIAM PILE ROGERS.

On Wednesday morning, at "Kingston Cottage," the residence of P. O'NEALE, Esq., after a long and painful illness, Mr. JAMES BASCOM, aged 31 years.

Figure 10 a) Page of *The Liberal* newspaper, 9 September 1854, showing marriage notice. (CO 33/12)
b) Notice of death of Henry Grannum, from *The Liberal*, 30 August 1854. (CO 33/12)

baptisms and burials: St George, 1739-1745 (ff 107-110); St Paul's, Falmouth, 1742-1745 (ff 111-112).

Barbados

1715-1716 CO 28/15
baptisms and burials: Christ Church (ff 95-97); St George (f 102); St John (f 103); St Andrew (f 105); St Joseph (ff 107-109); and St Peter (ff 110-114). Printed in John Camden Hotten, *The Original Lists of Persons of Quality* (Baltimore, Genealogical Publishing Co, Inc, 1980).

Jamaica

1821-1825 CO 137/162, March
returns of slave marriages in Portland, St James, St Catherine, Kingston and Manchester.

Montserrat

1721-1729 CO 152/18
baptisms and burials: St Anthony, 1723-1729 (ff 51-57); St George (ff 57-61); and St Peter (ff 61-63).
marriages: St Patrick (f 63); St Anthony (ff 64-65); St George (ff 65-66); and St Peter (ff 66-67).

1739-1745 CO 152/25
baptisms and burials: various parishes (f 137).

Nevis

1726-1727 CO 152/16
baptisms and burials: St Paul (f 341).

1733-1734 CO 152/21
baptisms and burials: St John (f 163); St Thomas (ff 163-164); St George (f 164).

1740-1745 CO 152/25
baptisms and burials: St James (ff 114-115).

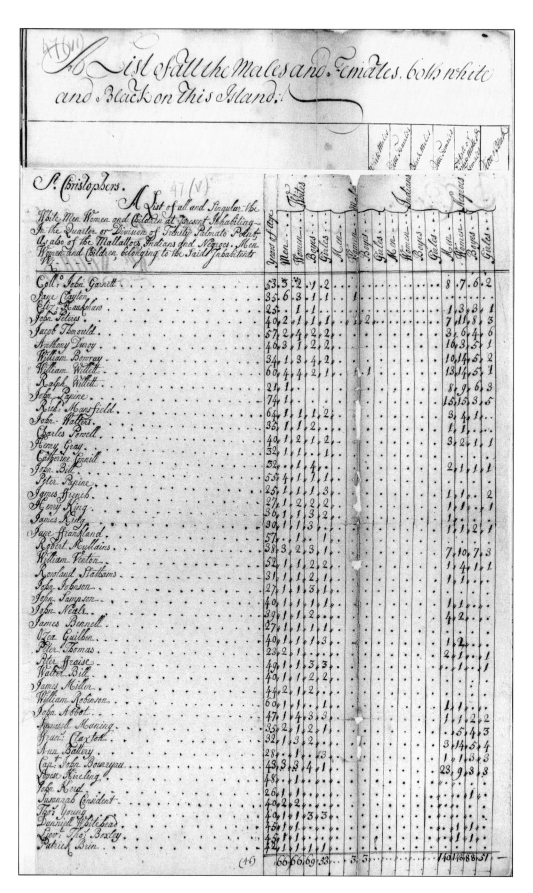

Figure 11   St Christopher: list of inhabitants, 1707 (CO 152/7 f 47v)

St Christopher

1721-1730 CO 152/18
baptisms and burials: Christ Church, Nichola Town (ff 25-27); St John, Cabosaterre (f 34); and St Mary Cayon (ff 36-38).

1733-1734 CO 152/18
baptisms and burials: Christ Church, Nichola Town (ff 132, 134); St Mary Cayon (ff 133, 135); St George, Basseterre (ff 136-143); St Ann, Sandy Point (ff 143-144, 147-148).

1738-1745 CO 152/25
baptisms, marriages and burials: St Mary Cayon (ff 118-121).
baptisms and burials: St George, Basseterre, 1743-1745 (ff 123-136).

5.2 Censuses and other listings

The English government was interested in colonial populations long before it showed an interest in its own population. Prior to 1670 few returns were made, but with the creation of the Council for Foreign Plantations in 1670, regular reports from the colonies were sought. The information required was the numbers of men and women, children and adults, masters and servants, and free persons and slaves, the annual growth of the population, and the number in the militia. This information was required so that the government could record not only the growth of the new colonies, but also their economic wealth, and more importantly their military strength. Some colonial governors sent regular returns, others waited for specific requests.

The majority of censuses which were returned to London were in the form of head-counts of varying information. The most simple returns gave only the total population, the numbers of males and females and degrees of freedom. In more detailed censuses the population was broken down into sex, age group, marital status, degrees of freedom, colour or race. These are to be found among the original correspondence of the individual colonies, merely as a list or maybe with printed demographic analysis. Statistical counts of the population occur in the blue books of statistics and government gazettes for the individual colonies, and are occasionally printed in the British Parliamentary Papers.

I have compiled a detailed list of West Indian censuses, and three from Sierra Leone, from records held in the PRO, which give at least the name of the head of household. Details of pre-1776 American colonial censuses, with demographic analyses, are described in Robert V Wells, *The Population of the British Colonies in America before 1776* (Princeton University Press, 1975). It is possible that other census returns, especially any for the nineteenth and twentieth centuries, are to be found in the islands' own archives. If returns which list the inhabitants have been kept it is possible that these will be closed for one hundred years.

The records in the PRO include many other types of returns of populations: for example, petitions from prominent landowners, tax returns, and electoral registers. The returns are to be found in the original correspondence and government gazettes for the individual colonies (some are listed in Appendix 2).

5.2.1 List of West Indian nominal censuses

Anguilla

1716   CO 152/11, f 56
Printed in *Caribbeana*, Vol 3, p 255.

1717   CO 152/12, no 67 (iv).

Antigua

1677/8   CO 1/42, ff 229-241
Indicates whether English, Irish, Scottish, French or Dutch.
Printed in Vere Langford Oliver, *History of the Island Antigua* (1894), vol 1, p lviii.

1753   CO 152/27, ff 271-303
Printed in Vere Langford Oliver, *History of the Island Antigua* (1894), vol 1, p cix.

1784   CO 10/2
Inhabitants of the parish of Riviere du Loup in the district of Three Rivers (Antigua or Montserrat?). Married men, age, profession and numbers in household, women, children, servants, slaves, amount of land, livestock [in French].

Bahamas

1731   CO 23/3, ff 4-10.

1734   CO 23/3, ff 129-132.

Barbados

1679/80   CO 1/44, no 47, i-xxii
Printed in John Camden Hotten, *Original Lists of Persons of Quality* (Baltimore, Genealogical Publishing Co, Inc, 1980), and James C Brandow, *Omitted Chapters from Hotten* (Baltimore, Genealogical Publishing Co, Inc, 1982) .

1715   CO 28/16, no 2
Some of the parishes list all white inhabitants with their ages.
The parishes of St Michael, Christchurch and St George are printed in the *Journal of the Barbados Museum and Historical Society*, vol IV, p 72.

Carriacou

c. 1767   CO 101/11, f 230
Householder, numbers of English overseers, French overseers and slaves, quantity of land, taxes.

Grenada

1772   CO 101/5, ff 147-151
List of landholders, the numbers in the household, acreage, negroes, types of crops and mills.

Jamaica

1680   CO 1/45, ff 96-109
Inhabitants of Port Royal and St Johns only.

1754   CO 137/28, pp 191-196
St Andrews' parish. Plantation, landholder, numbers of acres, types of crops, livestock, etc, numbers of slaves.

1754   CO 142/31
List of landholders with number of acres, taken from the Quit Rent Books.

1831   CO 140/121, pp 353-378
Return of maroons of Moore-town, Charlestown, Scot's Hall and Accompong.
Name and age, some give colour and comments such as son of., return of
slaves belonging to the maroons.

Montserrat

1677/8   CO 1/42, ff 218-228
Indicates whether English, Irish, Scottish, French or Dutch.
Printed in *Caribbeana*, vol 2, p 318.

1729   EXT 1/258 (extracted from CO 152/18)
Printed in *Caribbeana*, vol 4, p 302.

Nevis

1677/8   CO 1/42, ff 201-217
Indicates whether English, Irish, Scottish, French or Dutch.
Printed in *Caribbeana*, vol 3, p 27.

1707   CO 152/7, f 47
Printed in *Caribbeana*, vol 3, p 255.

St Christopher

1677/8   CO 1/42, ff 195-200
Indicates whether English, Irish, Scottish, French or Dutch.
Printed in *Caribbeana*, vol 2, p 68.

1707   CO 152/7, f 47
Includes age of head of household.
Printed in *Caribbeana*, vol 3, p 132.

1711   CO 152/9, ff 305-315.

St Eustatius

1781   CO 318/8, ff 60-82
List of all burghers resident in the island of St Eustatius.

St Lucia

1811   CO 253/7 [in French].

Sierra Leone

1802   WO 1/352
Return of Nova Scotians and Maroons.

1831   CO 267/111
A detailed census in two parts: (1) Liberated Africans, discharged soldiers with occupation and the numbers of others in the household; (2) arranged on printed forms: name, occupation, description (white, mulatto, colonial residents and free-born blacks), discharged soldier, Liberated African, native stranger.

1833   CO 267/127
Details as above. Includes in the first part of the volume the numbers of liberated slaves per year, listed by vessel.

Spanish Town

1717   CO 152/12, no 67 (vi)
Includes nationality.

Surinam

1811   CO 278/15-27
Slave, black, coloured, white and free populations are distinguished.

Tobago

1770   CO 101/14, ff 126-127.

1751   CO 285/2, ff 77-78
Listing of French inhabitants of Little Tobago to Roddey by P Drummond of HMS *Tavistock*.

Tortola

1717   CO 152/12, no 67 (viii)
Includes country of origin.

5.3 Wills

Probate of wills was traditionally carried out by ecclesiastical courts. Most wills in the West Indies would have been handled by the local church courts. However, British subjects dying abroad or at sea with personal estates in England or Wales, and members of the navy and army, would have had their wills proved in the Prerogative Court of Canterbury (PCC).

The ecclesiastical courts in Britain were abolished under the Probate Act 1857 with effect from 12 January 1858, and probate was taken over by the Court of Probate, now the Principal Registry of the Family Division. Wills later than this date are held at the Principal Registry, Somerset House, The Strand, London WC2R 1LP.

The series of PCC records begin in 1383 for wills and 1559 for administrations. Administrations are letters granting estate to the next of kin, or creditors, in cases where a will was not made. There are chronological indexes by initial letter of surname to wills and administrations. Alphabetical indexes to the wills, 1383-1700, and administrations, 1559-1660, have been published by the British Records Association. The Society of Genealogists has published an index to wills, 1750-1800, and they are currently working on administrations.

Registered copy wills, 1383-1858 (PROB 11) are available on microfilm, as are the grants of administration, 1559-1858 (PROB 6). Original wills (PROB 10) currently require five working days notice to produce. Copy wills were made by PCC clerks after probate, and include details of the probate; original wills are those of the testators, and include their signature.

Wills usually give details of the testators' immediate family and their bequests, together with some information about the property. Slaves are often mentioned in West Indian wills. Letters of administration, however, give very little information except that of the administrator, or administratrix. Lists of West Indian wills proved in the PCC for the period 1628-1816 are to be found in *Caribbeana*, volumes 2-5.

Inventories are lists of the testator's estate detailing its value. Since they were lists of the testator's property they may include lists of slaves. Up to 1722 it was obligatory for every executor or administrator to return into the court's

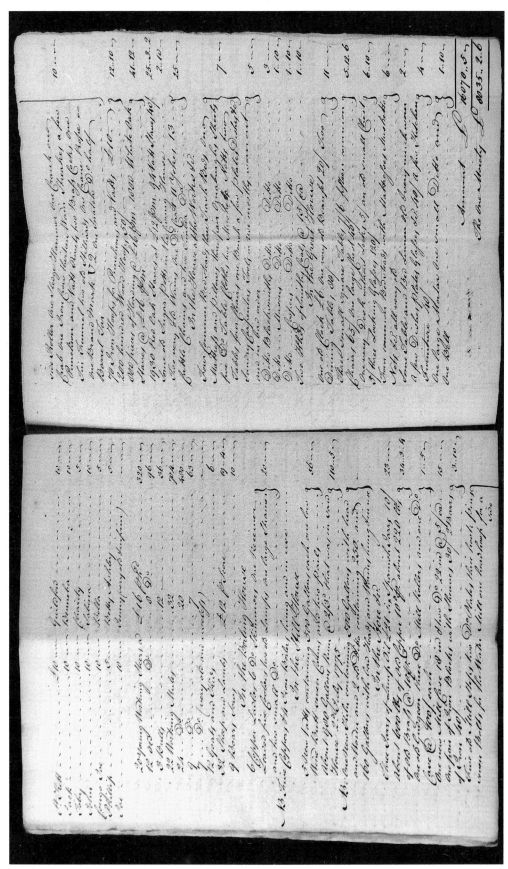

Figure 12   Inventory of Samuel Smith, 1777, showing slaves listed as goods.
                   (PROB 31/647/422)

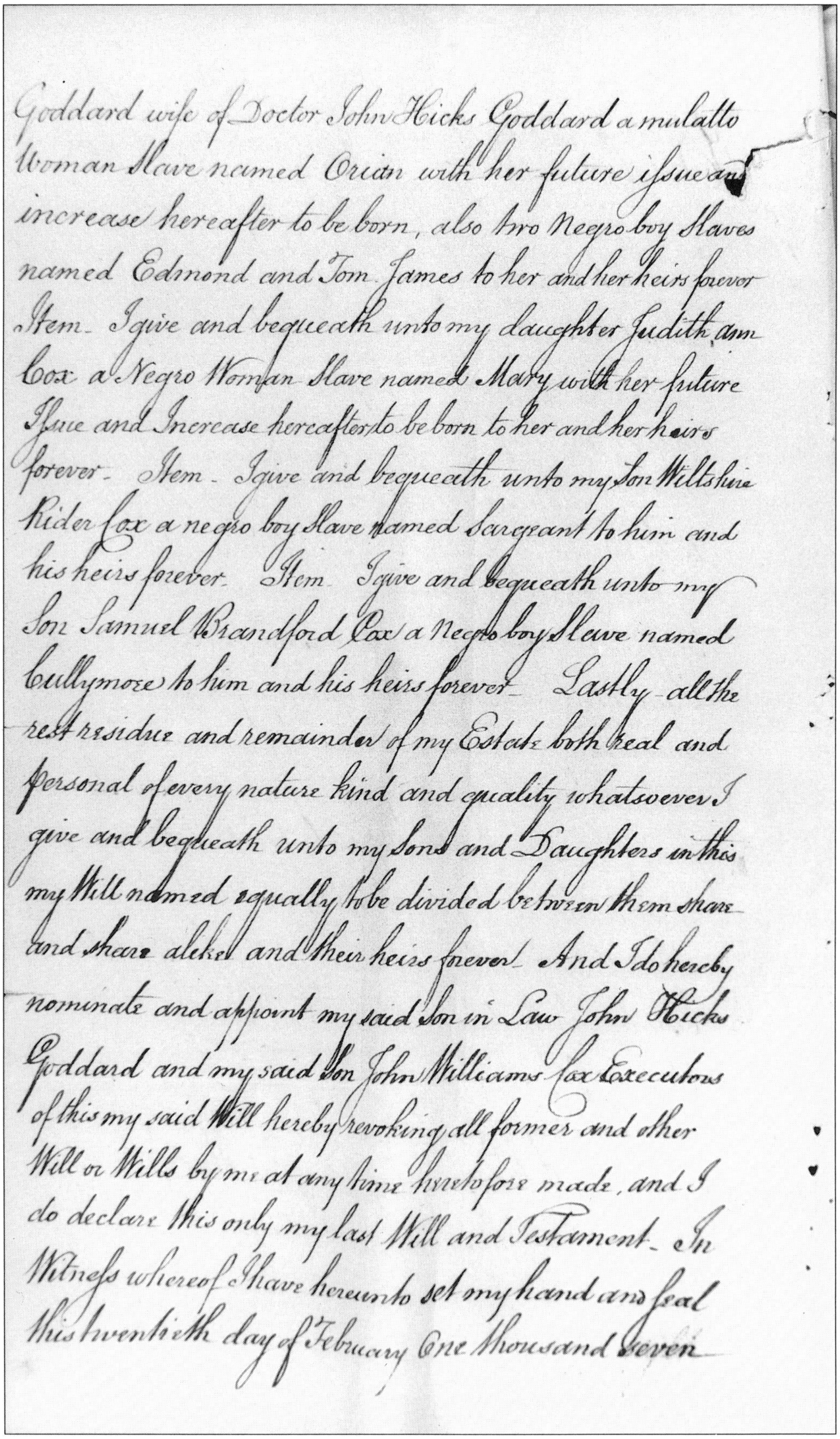

Goddard wife of Doctor John Hicks Goddard a mulatto
Woman Slave named Orian with her future issue and
increase hereafter to be born, also two Negro boy Slaves
named Edmond and Tom James to her and her heirs forever
Item. I give and bequeath unto my daughter Judith Ann
Cox a Negro Woman Slave named Mary with her future
Issue and Increase hereafter to be born to her and her heirs
forever. Item. I give and bequeath unto my Son Wiltshire
Rider Cox a negro boy Slave named Sargeant to him and
his heirs forever. Item. I give and bequeath unto my
Son Samuel Brandford Cox a Negro boy Slave named
Cullymore to him and his heirs forever. Lastly all the
rest residue and remainder of my Estate both real and
personal of every nature kind and quality whatsoever I
give and bequeath unto my Sons and Daughters in this
my Will named equally to be divided between them share
and share alike and their heirs forever. And I do hereby
nominate and appoint my said Son in Law John Hicks
Goddard and my said Son John Williams Cox Executors
of this my said Will hereby revoking all former and other
Will or Wills by me at any time heretofore made, and I
do declare this only my last Will and Testament. In
Witness whereof I have hereunto set my hand and seal
this twentieth day of February One thousand seven

Figure 13 Will of Fearnot Cox, 1784, showing slaves being bequeathed to family members. (PROB 37/897)

registry an inventory of the deceased's goods. After this date inventories were only called for as exhibits in the PCC during litigation. PROB 4, 1661 to 1720, is the largest collection of inventories, and there is a card index to the deceased, as well as a topographical index. From 1722 some inventories are to be found in PROB 31, exhibits, and PROB 37, causes. These records may also contain original and copy wills, and other papers, from courts outside the PCC.

Most West Indian wills were proved locally, and should survive in the relevant archive. Following a French invasion of St Christopher and Nevis in 1711, powers of attorney were granted for payment of compensation. Copies of these powers, 1712-1720, together with a number of wills, are in CO 243/4-5. Lists of wills proved and letters of administration sometimes occur in the government gazettes.

Further reading:

PRO Records Information Leaflets

31 - *Probate Records*

Tracing Your Ancestors, section 6

Coldham, Peter Wilson, *American Wills Proved in London 1611-1775* (Baltimore, Genealogical Publishing Co, Inc, 1992).

Coldham, Peter Wilson, *American Wills & Administrations in the Prerogative Court of Canterbury 1610-1857* (Baltimore, Genealogical Publishing Co, Inc, 1989).

Cox, Jane, *Wills, Inventories and Death Duties. The Records of the Prerogative Court of Canterbury and the Estate Duty Office. A Provisional Guide* (London, Public Record Office, 1988).

Gibson, J S W, *A simplified guide to probate jurisdictions: where to look for wills*, 3rd edn (Federation of Family History Societies, 1986).

Oliver, Vere Langford, ed, *Caribbeana*, 6 vols (1910-1919). Volumes 2 to 5 contain lists of Prerogative Court of Canterbury (PCC) wills, 1628-1816, and some abstracts of early PCC wills for Nevis and St Kitts. Volumes 1 and 2 contain lists of Jamaican wills, and vols 4 and 5 have lists of Barbadian wills.

Chapter 6: Land and Property

6.1 Land grants

In early colonial America the ownership of the land was vested in the crown by right of discovery and settlement by its subjects. The crown granted land to companies and to proprietors to organize settlement. During the Commonwealth, 1649 to 1660, most of the colonies reverted to the crown which granted land through its appointed governors.

During the eighteenth century many colonies of European powers were occupied by and then ceded to Britain, among them Dominica, Grenada, Trinidad, Tobago, British Guiana, St Vincent, and the French portion of St Christopher. The British authorities sought to encourage British settlement, and began to require returns to be made of lands granted, purchased, or rented on many of these islands. Returns were also made of non-British proprietors.

Most land grants were recorded locally rather than in London, and these survive in the former colonies. Those in the PRO are to be found among the Colonial Office records (section 3). Lands granted by the governor can be found in the original correspondence and the entry books for each colony. Lands granted through local government, such as the legislative assemblies of council, are in sessional papers. From the mid-1800s the government gazettes are a rich source of information, and contain notices for sales of crown land, auction notices for plantations, arrears of rent for government properties, land and house tax defaulters, land rolls, electoral lists, grants of land, grants of homesteads, and applications for land claims.

6.1.1 Lists of land grants

Bahamas

1734   CO 23/3, ff 180-181
An account of taxes on plots of land in the Town of Nassau.

1847   CO 23/125
Return of land grants, 1841-1846.

A List of such Contracts made by the Commissioners for Sale of Lands in St Christophers that formerly belonged to the French, as have been confirmed by the Commissioners of his Majt Treasury.

252

248

Purchasers Names	Quantities purchased				In what parts of the Island.
	Acres	Roods	Perches	Square Feet	
Patrick Blake Esqr	22		17		Basse Terre Quarter
Ditto	140	3	31		Cabeca Terre Quarter
Ditto	35		7		Basse Terre Quarter
Ditto				3187	Basse Terre Town
James Malliard	39	1	26		Cabeca Terre Quarter
Charles Payne Esqr	199		14		Ditto
John Douglas Esqr	200				Basse Terre Quarter
Dame Frances Stapleton	200				Ditto
Ditto				10608	Basse Terre Town
Theodore Vanelburgh Georges	78		28		Cabeca Terre Quarter
Peter Soulegre Esqr	146	3	19		Ditto
Ditto	53		21		Ditto
William McDowal Esqr	200				Basse Terre Quarter
Ditto				2580	Basse Terre Town
James Gordon Esqr	119	1	10		Basse Terre Quarter
James Milliken Esqr	200				Ditto
Ditto				5225	Basse Terre Town
Peter Salvetat Esqr	67	3	13		Cabeca Terre Quarter
Isaac Wilson				4365	Basse Terre Town
John Douglas Esqr				2129	Ditto
Richard Wilson	54		31		Basse Terre Quarter
Thomas Butler Esqr				4913	Deep Bay Town
John Orton	60		12		in Basse Terre Quarter
Edward Warner Esqr	40	2	13		Cabeca Terre Quarter
Drewry Ottley Esqr				8070	Basse Terre Town
John Spooner Esqr	78	1	34		Basse Terre Quarter
Charles Bym Esqr	108	3	8		Ditto
Timothy Hare Esqr				24328	Basse Terre Town
Nathaniel Parson Esqr				9240	Ditto
John Newth Esqr				10825	Ditto
Lawford Cole Esqr				10855	Ditto
George Taylour junr	129	3	20		Cabeca Terre Quarter
The Revd Mr Daniel Burchall	66	2	32		Ditto
Drewry Ottley Esqr	143	2	17		Basse Terre Quarter
Richard Howland				3660	Basse Terre Town
Mathew Mills Esqr				2700	Ditto
Anne Freeman				8425	Ditto

251

Figure 14   St Christopher: list of land that formerly belonged to the French. (T 1/275, f 248)

Belize (*formerly* **British Honduras**)

no date   WO 55/1815
Names of persons who have grants of land in George Town (near Cala Font)
Honduras.

Ceded Islands (Grenada, Tobago, Dominica, and St Vincent)

1765-1766   CO 76/9
Dominica and St Vincent: Register of grants of land.

1766   CO 101/1, ff 279-281
Docket register of plantation grants in the islands of Dominica, St Vincent
and Tobago.

1765-1767   CO 101/11
Docket register of plantation grants.
ff 209, 413 - Tobago
ff 212-217, 411-415 - St Vincent
ff 219-222, 413 - Dominica

1764-1797   CO 106/9-12
Sale of lands in the Ceded Islands.

Dominica
see also **Ceded Islands**

1766   T 1/453, ff 153-164
An account of lands granted on lease by the Commissioners to the French
inhabitants of Dominica.

1790-1803   CO 71/31
Includes returns of quit rents.

Grenada

1762-1764   CO 101/1, ff 245-246
A list of sale of town lots in St George.

Guyana (*formerly* **British Guiana**)

1819 CO 111/28
Lists of Dutch proprietors of plantations in Demerara, Essequibo and Berbice
[in Dutch].

1735-1755   CO 116/73, 75, 76
Berbice: grants of land [in Dutch].

1737-1763   CO 116/78
Berbice: mortgages [in Dutch].

Jamaica

1735-1754   CO 137/28, pp 197-203, 225-249
Return of land grants.

1805-1824   CO 137/162, Jan
Return of land grants.

St Christopher

1721   CO 152/13, ff 253-256
List of present possessors of the French land in Basseterre and Cabesterre divisions.

1729   T 1/275, ff 248-249
A list of contracts made by the Commissioners for Sale of Lands in St Christopher's that formerly belonged to the French.

St Vincent
see also **Ceded Islands**

1766   T 1/453, f 164
account of one fourth crops reaped from estates of which temporary possession was granted by the Commissioners in 1765.

ff 168-170
account of the French Inhabitants of St Vincent whose claims are allowed by the Commissioners and who paid their fines in May 1766.

Surinam

1805   WO 1/149, pp 307-357
List of plantation owners.

Tobago
see **Ceded Islands**

Trinidad

1814   CO 295/35
Abstract of all grants of land made by the Spanish government and all permissions of occupancy or petitions of grants from the Capitulation, 14 June 1813.

Further reading

PRO Records Information Leaflets

23 - *Records of the American and West Indian Colonies before 1782*

Barck Jnr, O T, and Lefler, H T, *Colonial America* (Collier, 1968)

6.2 Maps and plans

The PRO holds numerous maps and plans relating to the West Indies, and the individual colonies. The most important collections are CO 700, 1595-1909, and CO 1042, 1779-1947, for the Colonial Office, and WO 78, 1627-1953, for the War Office. Maps can also be found in the Colonial Office records for the colony, especially among the original correspondence records. Many of these are described in *Maps and Plans in the Public Record Office, II: America and the West Indies*. There are a card catalogue and printed supplementary catalogues in the Map Room, Kew. However, only a small percentage of the maps and plans held in the PRO have been catalogued.

Maps of the islands can give a lot of information about the landowners. Plantations which were often named after the owner are listed. Many maps were produced under subscription, and these include lists of the subscribers with their addresses. Some include the names of landowners: for example, the plan of St George's, Grenada, surveyed by the Commissioners for the Sale and Disposal of His Majesty's Lands, 1765 (CO 700/Grenada/5) identifies each parcel of land and lists the proprietor; many of the owners are included in the list of town lots granted by Governor Smith between 1762 and 1764 (CO 101/1, ff 245-246).

Further reading

PRO Records Information Leaflets

91 - *Maps in the Public Record Office*

Penfold, P A, ed, *Maps and Plans in the Public Record Office, II:
  America and the West Indies* (London, HMSO, 1974).

6.3 Plantation records

The PRO holds very few records of plantations because they are private papers.
Surviving records can be found in a variety of places which reflect the
movements of the owner. For example, where the owners were absentee
landlords and resided in Britain, or eventually returned to Britain, these records
may survive in a British local record office. The papers of families which
remained in the colony may survive in that country's archive. It is also possible
that the records may still remain with the family who owned, or managed, the
estate. The Royal Commission on Historical Manuscripts, Quality House,
Quality Court, Chancery Lane, London WC2A 1HP, may be able to advise on
the whereabouts of surviving papers in Britain.

The equity side of the Court of Chancery dealt with a large and varied range of
disputes such as inheritance, lands, debts, bankruptcy, and marriage settlement.
Papers such as accounts, deeds, journals, and correspondence were provided
as evidence in the Court of Chancery. Those that were not returned to, or
reclaimed by, the owner have survived as Chancery Masters Exhibits (C 103-
C 114). The few collections which the PRO holds of plantations occur because
the estate, or owner, was involved in litigation. Many of these records include
lists of slaves, and plantation accounts.

Other plantation records are found among the records of the West Indian
Incumbered Estates Commission, 1770-1893 (CO 441). This Commission was
set up under the West India Incumbered Estates Act 1854, to investigate estates
which had become overburdened by mortgages, and in some cases to sell them.
The Commission was in existence until 1892, and sold 382 estates. Some were
sold by agents locally on the islands, but the vast majority (350) were sold in

London. CO 441 contains the records of the Commission and the papers of 205 estates, the majority in Jamaica and Antigua. The records are arranged by date of sale, and contain transfer of mortgages, newspapers advertising the sale, and various accounts and deeds, including plans. Many of the records are from the late eighteenth and early nineteenth centuries, and some include lists of slaves.

Further reading

PRO Records Information Leaflet

30 - *Chancery Proceedings (Equity suits)*

Tracing Your Ancestors, section 47

Walne, Peter, ed, *A Guide to Manuscript Sources for the History of Latin America and the Caribbean in the British Isles* (Oxford University Press, 1973).

Chapter 7: Military and Related Records

There was almost constant warfare between the European powers in the West Indies, even when they were at peace in Europe. To protect her colonies Britain had a permanent military presence. Every colony possessed local militia; troops of the established army were based on the islands; and the Royal Navy patrolled the seas, moving troops, and protecting convoys and the colonies from pirates and enemies. The merchant navy transported goods between Europe and the colonies, including slaves, and was a source of manpower for the Royal Navy. Many soldiers and sailors who served in the West Indies did not return to Britain: thousands died through tropical diseases and through warfare; many deserted; and some remained in the colonies after discharge.

I will only briefly describe the records of the services because they are better described elsewhere (see further reading), but I will highlight records which are pertinent to the West Indies.

7.1 Army

The army was permanently stationed in the West Indies; each of the established regiments did a tour of duty, and every island had a barracks. The forces were made up predominantly of recruits from Britain, with a small number of other Europeans, and some local men. Many foreign regiments on British pay also served in the West Indies, especially during the American War of Independence and the French Revolutionary and Napoleonic Wars.

Officers: The starting point for information about officers is the *Army List* which records the officer's regiment, and the dates of his commission. The manuscript army lists, 1702-1752, are in WO 64. From 1754 they are published and are available in the Reference Room at Kew. Personal details of officers can be found among the Commander-in-Chief's memoranda in WO 31, 1793-1870, and in the widows' pension applications among the miscellaneous certificates in WO 42, 1755-1908. There is an incomplete run of officers' services in WO 25 for various periods between 1808 and 1872, and in WO 76 for various periods between 1829 and 1919. There is an incomplete nominal card index to these returns in the Reference Room.

Other ranks: The most detailed record of a soldier's service is provided by the attestation and discharge papers in WO 97 for those soldiers who were discharged to pension between 1760 and 1913. These record the place of birth, age on enlistment, place of enlistment, a physical description, and the record of service. From 1883 details of next of kin, wife and children are given. WO 97 is in three series: 1756-1854 and 1855-1872, arranged alphabetically by surname under the regiment; 1873-1882, alphabetically by name under the type of corps (infantry, cavalry, artillery); and 1883-1913, alphabetically by surname. The third group includes not only those discharged to pension but also those discharged after limited engagements, or by purchase. An index to the first series, 1760-1854, is being compiled by the Friends of the Public Record Office. Print-outs are available in the Reference Room.

If the attestation and discharge papers do not survive then details of a soldier's service can be obtained by a search of the musters and pay lists. It is important to know the regiment in which he served because these are arranged by regiment. The musters for infantry and cavalry, 1740-1878, are in WO 12; artillery, 1708-1878, WO 10; and engineers, 1816-1878, WO 11. From 1878 until 1898 they are all in WO 16. These volumes can be used to trace enlistment, movements, and discharge or death, of soldiers. On enlistment the pay book should give the age and place of birth. From 1868 details of marriages with the numbers and ages of children are shown. The description books in WO 25 give the physical description of soldiers on enlistment; for the West Indian regiments these sometimes include tribal markings.

Until 1855 the artillery and engineers were the responsibility of the Board of Ordnance. Some musters and description books are in WO 54 and records of service are preserved in WO 69.

If you do not know the regiment, but have information such as a date and a place, then you can identify possible regiments by using the regimental returns in WO 17, WO 73 and WO 379. A useful guide to the stations of regiments is John M Kitzmiller, *In Search of the 'Forlorn Hope'*, 2 vols (Utah, Manuscript Publishing Foundation, 1988).

Soldiers who were discharged after completing an agreed term of service or as invalids were entitled to a pension. The Royal Hospital Chelsea administered pensions for the army and the records include those who discharged and received pensions in the West Indies. The out-pension admission books are arranged chronologically by the date of the examination for pension and are in two series: pensions awarded for disability, 1715-1913 (WO 116); and pensions awarded for length of service, 1823-1920 (WO 117). Pension registers (WO 22, 1845-1880, and WO 23, 1817-1903) include pensions awarded in the colonies, and to black pensioners. These registers are arranged by colony and give details of payment, and the date of death if it occurred within the period of the register. Sometimes the regiment is noted, which will aid research in the pay lists and in the soldiers' documents.

The service records for officers and soldiers who fought during and after the First World War are held by the Ministry of Defence, CS(R)2b, Bourne Avenue, Hayes, Middlesex UB3 1RF. They will give only brief details to the soldier, or to the official next of kin. Enquirers must apply in writing. Their record centre was bombed during the Second World War and a significant proportion of the service records for the First World War were destroyed or badly damaged. I have been advised that unfortunately those for the British West India Regiment were among those destroyed.

The PRO holds the campaign medal rolls, unit war diaries, and selected medical records for the First World War. The medal rolls (WO 329) contain the names of some five million soldiers who received a service medal. The index is available on microfiche in the Microfilm Reading Room. War diaries (WO 95) are arranged by theatre of war and then hierarchically by division, brigade, etc; they rarely name individuals apart from officers. Medical records of the field medical centres (MH 106) contain admissions and discharges with brief details of the medical condition.

7.1.1 West Indian regiments

The West India regiments were raised in 1795 as a black corps to complement the European regiments. The troops were predominantly black with white officers and non-commissioned officers (NCOs), although some blacks did rise to become NCOs. The origin of these regiments was the Carolina Black Corps which was a loyalist troop raised during the American Revolution. After the revolution the Carolina Black Corps formed various black pioneer, garrison, and infantry corps serving in the West Indies. Supplementing these corps were locally raised black pioneer and ranger corps. These corps were not enough to form the twelve West India regiments, so officials bought slaves. These were first bought from existing slave owners, but later they were bought directly from slave ships. It is estimated that from 1795 to 1807 the British army bought seven per cent of all slaves sold in the West Indies.

In 1807 the slave trade was made illegal, and all of the former military slaves were emancipated, but remained in the army. The recruiters turned to Liberated Africans seized from illegal traders by Customs officials and the Royal Navy, and established recruiting depots in ports such as Freetown, Sierra Leone and Havana. Many were attested for 'Unlimited Service', ie for life. Other groups enlisted included soldiers from the Bourbon Regiment, from Mauritius, which was disbanded in 1816; blacks from Santo Domingo, Martinique and Guadeloupe; Europeans, from Belgium and Germany; and American slaves who enlisted during the Anglo-American War of 1812.

Other locally raised corps were garrison companies and the Military Labourers, many of whom were also slaves and Liberated Africans.

Many papers related to policy and the recruitment of black regiments are to be found among the records of the War Office and the Colonial Office. These are described in PRO List and Indexes vol LIII, *An Alphabetical Guide to certain War Office and other Military Records preserved in the Public Record Office.*

7.1.2 Records of West Indian regiments

T 1/664

> 1788 - List of black pioneers belonging to the Royal Artillery victualled at Grenada.
>
> 1788/9 - Musters of officers, soldiers, wives and children for the Black Dragoons, Black Artificers, Corps of Pioneers, Black Pioneers, 67th Rgt and 45th Rgt victualled at Grenada.

Musters and pay lists

WO 12/10698	1796	Dutch Battalion at Essequibo and Demerara
WO 12/10785	1813-1819	Black and Bahama Garrison Companies
WO 12/10917-10931	1837-1875	Military Labourers
WO 12/11040	1795	Santo Domingo Corps
WO 12/11064	1796	South American Rangers

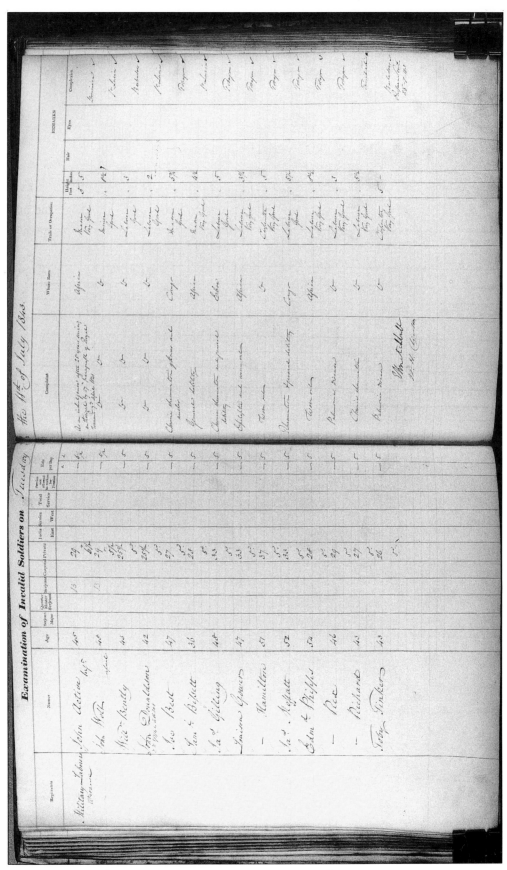

Figure 15   Army Pensioners: 'Negro Pensioners Book', 11 July 1843.
                 (WO 23/156),

WO 12/11233-11238	1805-1819	West Indian Rangers
WO 12/11239-11338	1795-1877	1st West India Regiment
WO 12/11339-11448	1795-1877	2nd West India Regiment
WO 12/11449-11508	1795-1870	3rd West India Regiment
WO 12/11509-11530	1797-1870	4th West India Regiment
WO 12/11531-11541	1797-1865	5th West India Regiment
WO 12/11542-11552	1796-1817	6th West India Regiment
WO 12/11553-11562	1795-1816	7th West India Regiment
WO 12/11563-11570	1798-1816	8th West India Regiment
WO 12/11571-11572	1799-1803	9th West India Regiment
WO 12/11573-11574	1799-1802	10th West India Regiment
WO 12/11575-11577	1799-1803	11th West India Regiment
WO 12/11578-11579	1799-1803	12th West India Regiment
WO 12/13289	1789-1791	Black Dragoons and others at Grenada
WO 16/2132-2152	1877-1888	1st battalion West India Regiment
WO 16/2153-2168	1877-1888	2nd battalion West India Regiment

Pension registers

WO 22/231-236	1845-1880	Black pensions
WO 22/248-257	1845-1875	Miscellaneous pensions in the colonies
WO 23/147-152	1817-1875	Pensions payable in the colonies
WO 23/153	1837-1840	Black and St Helena Corps pensioners
WO 23/154	c. 1837	Black pensioners
WO 23/156-159	1839-1879	Black pensioners
WO 23/160	1880-1903	Native and colonial pensioners
WO 43/108	1818	Lists of pensioners from the West India Regiments

Description Books

WO 25/644-645	1810-1831	2nd West India Regiment
WO 25/646-651	1826-1870	3rd West India Regiment
WO 25/652-655	1804-1819	4th West India Regiment
WO 25/656	1811-1817	5th West India Regiment
WO 25/657-659	1797-1817	6th West India Regiment
WO 25/660-662	1801-1817	7th West India Regiment
WO 25/663-665	1804-1819	West Indian Rangers

Casualty returns. These sometimes contain wills and copies of wills of deceased soldiers and inventories of their effects

WO 25/2196-2197	1817-1819	Bahama Garrison Company
WO 25/2244-2245	1809-1819	West Indian Rangers
WO 25/2246-2262	1809-1831	1-8 West India Regiments

Soldiers' documents

WO 97/1154	1760-1854	West Indian Rangers
WO 97/1155-1162	1760-1854	West India Regiments
WO 97/1183	1760-1854	Corps of Military Labourers

Further reading:

PRO Records Information Leaflets

59 - *British Army Records as sources for Biography and Genealogy*

Tracing Your Ancestors, section 18

Atkinson, C T, 'Foreign Regiments in the British Army 1793-1802', in *Journal of the Society for Army Historical Research*, vol 22, 1943/4.

Buckley, Roger Norman, *Slaves in Redcoats. The British West India Regiments, 1795-1815* (London, Yale University Press, 1979).

Fowler, Simon, *Army Records for Family Historians*, PRO Readers' Guide no 2 (London, PRO Publications, 1992).

Kieran, Brian L, *The Lawless Caymanas. A Story of Slavery, Freedom and the West India Regiment* (Bourne Press Ltd, 1992).

Kitzmiller, John M, *In Search of the 'Forlorn Hope'. A Comprehensive Guide to Locating British Regiments and their Records, 1640 to World War One*, 2 vols (Utah, Manuscript Publishing Foundation, 1988).

Public Record Office Lists and Indexes, vol LIII, *An Alphabetical Guide to certain War Office and other Military Records preserved in the Public Record Office.* (London, HMSO, 1931).

Watts, Christopher T and Watts, Michael J, *My Ancestor was in the British Army. How Can I Find Out More About Him?* (London, Society of Genealogists, 1992).

7.2 Militia

These were locally raised forces, formed to protect the colony itself. They were not expected to serve overseas. The PRO does not hold the records of

West Indian militia. However, the government gazettes among the Colonial Office records often contain lists of militia, and notices of promotion and retirement. Records of West Indian militia may survive in the islands' archives.

Further reading;

Thomas, Garth, *Records of the Militia from 1757*, PRO Readers' Guide no 3 (London, PRO Publications, 1993).

7.3 Royal Navy

The Royal Navy patrolled the islands, protecting them against invasions, pirates and privateers. They also protected merchant shipping between the colonies, and escorted convoys between Africa and the West Indies, and between the islands and Britain.

Officers: The starting point for tracing an officer's service is the typescript of Pitcairn-Jones' Commissioned Sea Officers' List, 1660-1815, issued by the National Maritime Museum, and the published *Navy List*, from 1782. Service registers were started during the nineteenth century, but few begin before the 1840s. The most important registers are ADM 196, which cover the 1770s to the 1920s. Indexes are in the Reference Room. Other returns and surveys of officers' services are in ADM 6, ADM 9, ADM 10, and ADM 11.

Other ranks: The PRO holds two series of registers for ratings: ADM 139, 1853-1872, and ADM 188, 1872-1892. These records give the date and place of birth. Certificates of service, 1802-1894, of warrant officers and ratings who applied for superannuation or admission to Greenwich Hospital are in ADM 29. Bound volumes of indexes to these records are in the Reference Room.

Prior to 1853, if there are no records in ADM 29, you must refer to the ships musters and pay lists, ADM 36-ADM 39, ADM 41, ADM 115 and ADM 117. These records cover the period 1667 to 1878 and are arranged by ship. The ship must be known, although if the place is known then it may be possible to identify the ships attached to the particular station, and then you can search the musters of each ship of that station.

The records for ratings who joined after 1892, and officers from the 1920s, are still held by the Ministry of Defence, who will give information only to the next of kin. Their addresses are:

1892-1939: MOD CS(R)2a, Bourne Avenue, Hayes, Middlesex UB3 1RF.

After 1939: PP1 A1, HMS Centurion, Grange Road, Gosport, Hampshire PO13 9XA.

Further reading:

PRO Records Information Leaflets

2 - *Admiralty Records as Sources for Biography and Genealogy*

Tracing Your Ancestors, section 19

Crewe, Duncan, *Yellow Jack and the Worm. British Naval Administration in the West Indies*, 1739-1748 (Liverpool University Press, 1993).

Rodger, N A M, *Naval Records for Genealogists*, PRO handbook no 22 (London, HMSO, 1988).

7.4 Dockyards

Most of the islands possessed naval dockyards, and the records include musters for Antigua, Barbados, Bermuda, Cape San Nicola Mole, Jamaica, and Martinique. Musters and pay lists for the larger yards are in the Yard Pay Books, ADM 42. Those for the minor yards and establishments are in ADM 32, ADM 36 and ADM 37. The main series of yard musters and lists survive into the mid-nineteenth century. The only later surviving records are the pensions registers in ADM 23, 1830-1926, and the Naval establishment: artificers and labourers civil pensions, PMG 25, 1836-1928.

The Bermudas were important as a naval and military station, and in 1810 work was begun on the naval station on Ireland Island, with the use of convict labour. Between 1824 and 1853 some nine thousand convicts were sent from Britain. It never became a penal settlement and they were able to return to

Britain on the completion of their sentence. The PRO holds baptisms, 1826-1946, and burials, 1826-1848, for the naval base at Ireland Island in ADM 6/434-436.

Further reading:

PRO Records Information Leaflets

15 - *Dockyard Employees: Documents in the PRO*

7.5 Royal Marines

The Royal Marines were the Royal Navy's soldiers, and the records for the Royal Marines survive in the Admiralty papers.

Officers: The records of Royal Marine officers are the same as those for the Royal Navy. From 1782 the published *Navy List* lists all commissioned Royal Marine officers by substantive rank and seniority, and the ships they were attached to. The *Army List* from 1740 also contains details of Royal Marine officers. The main series of service records is ADM 196, 1770s to 1920s. An index to the records of service of all Royal Marine officers commissioned between 1793 and 1970 is in ADM 313/110; a copy is available in the Reference Room.

Other ranks: The basic arrangement of records of other ranks' service is according to Division (Portsmouth, Chatham, Woolwich, or Plymouth). There are three main classes for records of service: description books, 1755-1940 (ADM 158); attestation forms, 1790-1925 (ADM 157); and records of service, from 1884 (ADM 159), which are closed for seventy-five years. Indexes to these records are in ADM 313, and there is a nominal card index to ADM 157 in the Reference Room. The effective and subsistence lists, 1688-1837 (ADM 96) list Royal Marines by company, and if it is known that a marine served on board a particular ship then the ships' musters in ADM 36-ADM 39 may contain some information.

For information on men who enlisted less than seventy-five years ago, enquiries should be made to the Drafting and Record Office, Royal Marines, HMS *Centurion*, Grange Road, Gosport, Hampshire PO13 9XA.

7.5.1 Colonial Marines

This corps was established during the Anglo-American War of 1812. The British forces offered to free any American slaves who joined the British. Many enlisted into the West India regiments and the Royal Navy, but some eight hundred formed the 3rd, or Colonial, battalion of the Royal Marines. Black refugees who were not enlisted into the services were discharged in Bermuda in March 1815. They settled later in Nova Scotia. The Colonial Marines were formed in May 1814, but most of the records do not begin until September 1814. There appear to be no attestation papers for these marines in ADM 157. The only lists of these marines are in the ships' musters (ADM 37), and in the effective and subsistence lists (ADM 96). The musters for HMS *Albion* in ADM 37/5005 and 5006 list Colonial Marines and black American refugees for April 1814 to March 1815. ADM 96/366 includes the lists for the Colonial Marines for 1816. The corps was disbanded in August 1816 in Bermuda and the marines were settled in the military townships in Trinidad.

Further reading:

PRO Records Information Leaflets

74 - *Royal Marine Records*

Tracing Your Ancestors, section 20

Thomas, Garth, *Records of the Royal Marines*, PRO Readers' Guide no 10 (London, PRO Publications, 1994).

Winks, Robin W, *The Blacks in Canada* (Yale University Press, 1971)

7.6 Merchant navy

The primary records for tracing a seaman's records lie in the musters and in the agreements and crew lists. These lists contain brief details of the voyage and the crew, including the previous ship on which they were employed. The agreements and crew lists include the town or county of birth. The musters run from 1747 to 1835, but only those for Shields, Dartmouth, Liverpool and Plymouth survive before 1800. Agreements and crew lists were started in 1835. All surviving musters and agreements before 1861 are in BT 98. Prior to 1854 they are arranged by the port of registration of the ship, after that date they are arranged by the ship's Official Number. Details of ships can be found in BT 111, *Lloyds Register* and the *Mercantile List*. Agreements later than 1860 are in BT 99, but the PRO only holds a ten per cent sample. The majority are in the possession of the Maritime History Group, Memorial University of Newfoundland, St John's A1C 5S7, Newfoundland, Canada. They will do a search for a fee if the name of the ship and the years of service are known.

Masters: in 1845 a system of voluntary examinations of competency for those intending to become masters or mates of foreign-going ships was introduced. It was made compulsory in 1850. The certificates were entered into registers in numerical order. The details entered were name, place and date of birth, register ticket number, rank examined for, or served in, and date and place of issue of ticket. Additional information can include names of ships sailed in, deaths, injuries and retirement. The indexes are in BT 127, which relate to BT 122-BT 126, and BT 128.

Seamen: between 1835 and 1856 the Board of Trade compiled several registers of seamen. The registers and indexes are in BT 112 to BT 120. The details given include name, date and place of birth, date and capacity of first going to sea, capacity since, and Royal Navy ship served in, home address.

Further reading:

PRO Records Information Leaflets

5 - *Records of the Registrar General of Shipping and Seamen*

Tracing Your Ancestors, section 25

Watts, Christopher T and Watts, Michael J, *My Ancestor was a Merchant Seaman. How Can I Find Out More About Him?* (London, Society of Genealogists, 1987).

Chapter 8: Slaves

Descendants of African slaves make up the majority of populations on all of the West Indian islands. On the British islands, slavery became an established form of labour from the 1640s when sugar cane was introduced into Barbados by Dutch merchants from Brazil. Sugar farming was physically demanding and mentally monotonous. Africans were used to tropical conditions, food, and disease, and were considered more suitable for this unpleasant form of agriculture than white indentured servants who had previously made up the labour market.

Slaves were chattel, that is they were personal property, they could be bought, sold, gifted, inherited, and bequeathed, according to the whims of their owner. Personal records of slaves are limited: they could not possess property, and in the British colonies they were actively discouraged from attending church. The records of slaves, their births and deaths, are to be found amongst the personal papers of their owners. For the most part records relating to slaves only occur when the slave, or owner, came to the attention of the crown, or to the colonial authorities. Many of the sources for slaves have already been discussed under records of the Colonial Office (section 3); slave trade (4.5); American Loyalists (4.7); births, marriages, and deaths (5.1); wills (5.3); and plantation records (6.3).

It is commonly believed that slaves took the surname of their owner, and that this will help in identifying records for family history. Although this did occur, it was not always the case. British slave law denied slaves surnames because they had no legal sire, and they were the property of their owner. On freedom, however, it seems that most slaves already possessed titles or surnames. Slaves often retained surnames from earlier owners which were carried by their descendants from one owner to the next. Gutman in *The Black Family in Slavery and Freedom* shows that American slaves were often known by the name of their original owner, who was not necessarily their last owner. A brief examination of the 'Book of Negroes' compiled by the British military authorities in 1783 of black refugees from the American Revolution (PRO 30/55/100, no 10427) reveals that the slaves rarely possessed the same surnames as their owners. This list has been indexed by the Guy Carleton Branch of the United Empire Loyalists' Association of Canada. The slave registers for St

Lucia and Trinidad show slaves listed in families with the children possessing the surname of their mother. This is possibly because the Catholic Church, in these former French and Spanish colonies, actively encouraged the baptism of slaves, and the slaves took their mother's surname. Surnames are uncommon in the registers for the established British colonies, which were Protestant and discouraged slaves from being baptised. Even after emancipation many slaves did not have surnames.

The most important records for slaves in the Public Record Office are those of the Colonial Office, the slave registry and the Slave Compensation Commission. Colonial Office records relating to slaves are numerous and include reports of slave rebellions; reports of protectors of slaves; inhabitants of workhouses; slaves being given their freedom (manumission); numbers of slaves being imported; and registration of slaves. Colonial newspapers contain notices of runaways which name the slave and often give a brief physical description, and notices for slave auctions.

8.1 Slave Registry and the Slave Compensation Commission

These records are the most important and most comprehensive for slave research in the British West Indies for the period 1812 to 1834.

The slave trade from Africa to British colonies was made illegal from 1807, but the trade between the islands did not become illegal until 1811. In 1812 Trinidad established a slave registry as a means to monitor legally held slaves. By 1817 most of the other islands had set up their own registries. The Slave Registration Act 1819 established a central registry of slaves in London, under the Commissioners of the Treasury. Under this act no slaves could be bought, sold, or inherited, if they had not first been entered in the appropriate island register. From 1820 governors also sent returns of manumissions, forfeited slaves and government slaves to the Colonial Office; these are to be found in the original correspondence classes.

The records of the central registry are in T 71, and continue until 1834 with the abolition of slavery. The registers are arranged by colony, and most contain indexes. Many of the volumes are arranged alphabetically by owner or estate. The registers contain much information on the slaves and their owners. For

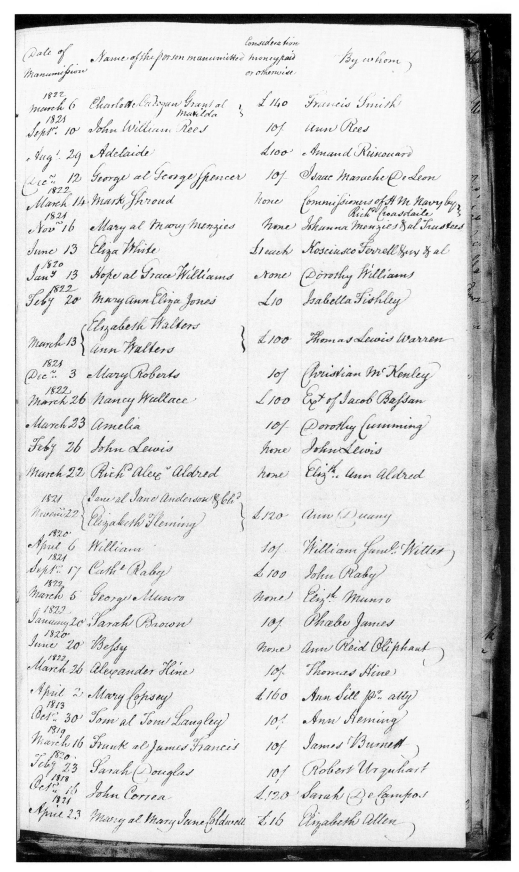

Figure 16   Manumission; list of persons manumitted in Jamaica, 1822.
(CO 137/162, March)

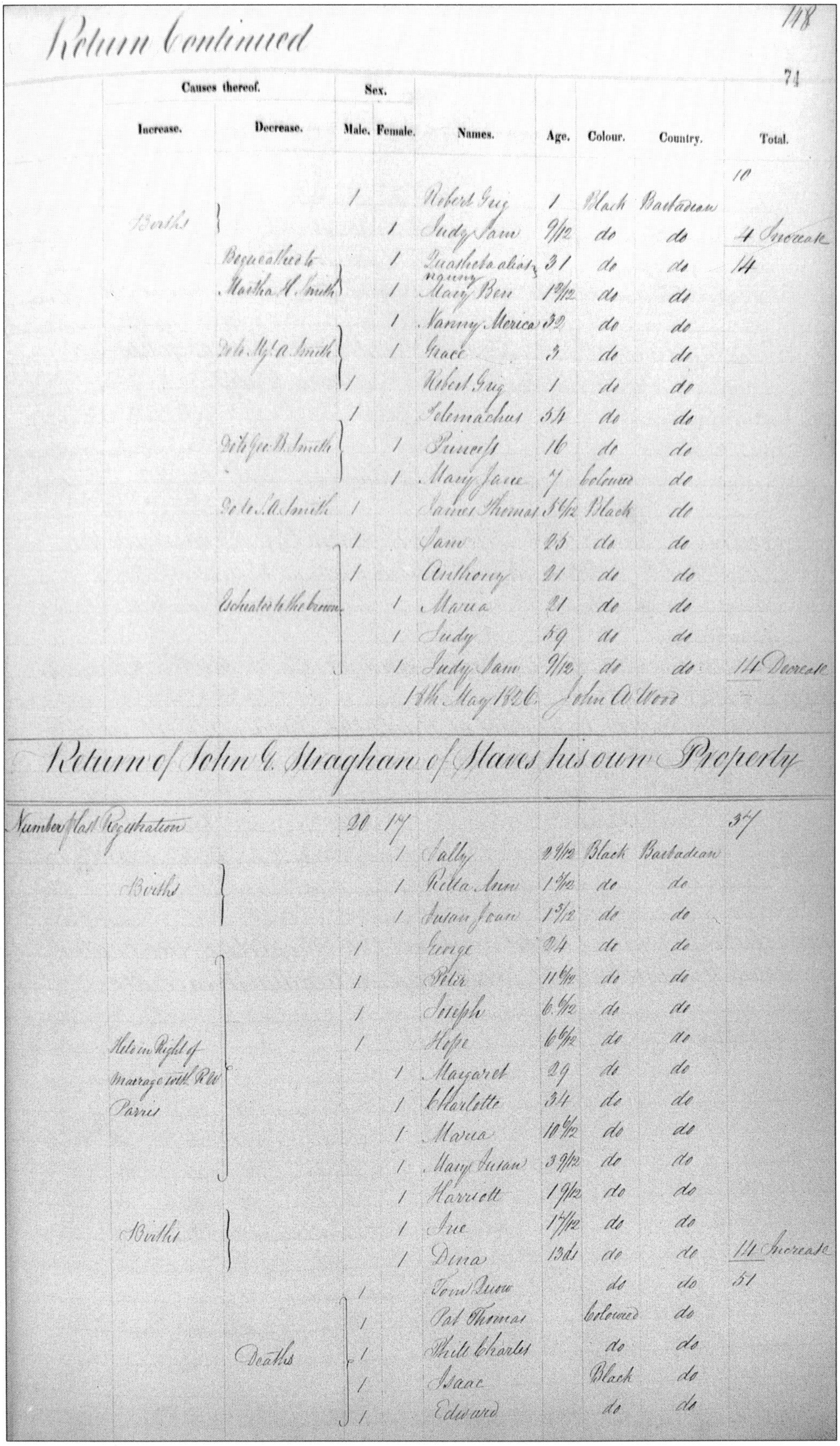

Return Continued 148 74

Increase	Decrease	Male	Female	Names	Age	Colour	Country	Total
								10
Births		1		Robert Grig	1	Black	Barbadian	
			1	Judy Sam	9/12	do	do	4 Increase
	Bequeathed to Martha A. Smith		1	Quasheba alias Nanny	31	do	do	14
			1	Mary Ben	1 9/12	do	do	
	Sold to Mrs A. Smith		1	Nanny Merica	32	do	do	
			1	Grace	3	do	do	
		1		Robert Grig	1	do	do	
		1		Telemachus	54	do	do	
	Sold to Geo B. Smith		1	Princess	16	do	do	
			1	Mary Jane	7	Coloured	do	
	Sold to S.A. Smith	1		James Thomas	5 5/12	Black	do	
	Escheated to the Crown	1		Sam	25	do	do	
		1		Anthony	21	do	do	
			1	Maria	21	do	do	
			1	Judy	59	do	do	
			1	Judy Sam	9/12	do	do	14 Decrease

18th May 1826. John A. Wood

Return of John G. Straghan of Slaves his own Property

Increase	Decrease	Male	Female	Names	Age	Colour	Country	Total
Number of last Registration		20	17					37
Births			1	Sally	2 9/12	Black	Barbadian	
			1	Rebecca Ann	1 5/12	do	do	
			1	Susan Joan	1 5/12	do	do	
Held in Right of marriage with R.W. Parris		1		George	24	do	do	
		1		Peter	11 6/12	do	do	
		1		Joseph	6 6/12	do	do	
		1		Hope	6 6/12	do	do	
			1	Margaret	29	do	do	
			1	Charlotte	34	do	do	
			1	Maria	10 6/12	do	do	
			1	Mary Susan	3 9/12	do	do	
			1	Harriett	1 9/12	do	do	
Births			1	Sue	1 7/12	do	do	
			1	Dina	13ds	do	do	14 Increase
	Deaths	1		Tom Quow		do	do	51
		1		Pol Thomas		Coloured	do	
		1		Phill Charles		do	do	
		1		Isaac		Black	do	
		1		Edward		do	do	

Figure 17 Slave register; St Joseph, Barbados 1826 showing an owner's marriage and death. (T 71/537, f 74)

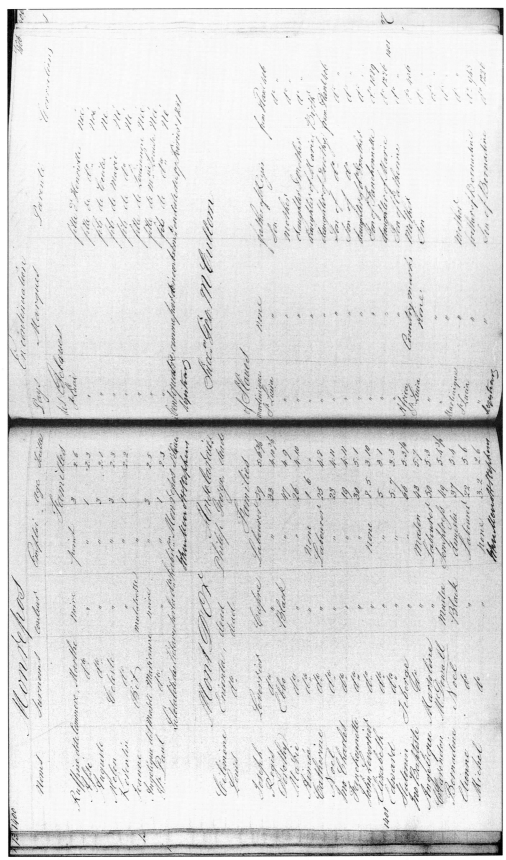

Figure 18   Slave register; St Lucia, 1831.Slaves of Monrepos plantation,
                   Mont D'Or, showing slave family with surnames. (T 71/388, p 1400)

slaves they give at least name, age, colour, and country of origin. They note increases and decreases on the last registration period, recording births and deaths, purchases, sales, inheritances and manumissions. For the owner they can be used to show deaths, marriages, and details of family members. Slaves were bequeathed, and inherited, they were often given 'in right of marriage' where the wife's slaves became the property of her husband's on marriage, and the wife is often named. Slaves of minors were registered by their guardians.

The information given in the registers differs between colonies. After the first registration most colonies only note increases and decreases in their numbers of slaves. Others, such as St Lucia and Bermuda, list all slaves. The mother's name is occasionally noted in the returns. Those for St Lucia are arranged by family and record other family members such as brothers, sisters, and cousins if on the same return. Fathers are rarely recorded.

Slavery was abolished in 1834, under the Abolition of Slavery Act 1833, and a sum of £20 million was provided to compensate slave owners. The records of the Slave Compensation Commission are in T 71 and contain information which was used to compensate slave owners on the abolition of slavery. The Commission was terminated in 1842, but one of the commissioners was appointed to adjudicate on outstanding claims. The National Debt Office dealt with payment of claims, and the records are in NDO 14, West Indies Slave Compensation. Other compensation returns are in AO 14/37-48.

The records of the slave compensation commissioners are arranged by colony and contain the following returns:

(i) **Valuers returns**: bound volumes of printed forms used for calculating compensation for slaves on 1 August 1834. The categories of slaves used for calculation were praedial (agricultural slaves); non-praedial (domestic slaves); children under the age of six; and the aged, diseased or otherwise non-effective. They may give the name of the estate.

(ii) **Registers of claims**: these are in claim number order, and show whether there was a claim or counter-claim. A claim was where the slave owners claimed for compensation; a counter-claim occurred where there was a dispute on the estate and other parties also claimed for compensation.

(iii) Indexes to claims: arranged by the initial letter of the surname, and give the surname, first names, the estate, the parish, and claim number.

(iv) Original claims and certificates: bound volumes in claim number order, with a copy certificate of claim and the original claim. These are signed and may include further details omitted from the registers, for example children born to slaves after the final registration.

(v) Counter-claims: loose papers with evidence used in counter-claims, they may include much family material.

(vi) Adjudication in contested claims: ledgers in claim number order, with the name of the counter-claim, date of deeds, subject of counter-claim, name of claimant, and remarks.

(vii) Certificates and awards: copy certificates issued by the compensation commissioners.

(viii) Parliamentary returns of awards: these were presented to Parliament and contain the amount paid. The volumes consist of two lists: List A, uncontested claims; and List B, litigated claims. List A gives the date of award, claim number, party to whom payment was awarded, number of slaves, and the sum payable. List B contains the same information as List A but does not include the number of slaves. The returns are in claim number order.

(ix) Exhibits: sales of slaves, 1823-1830, which were used by the commissioners to assess the values of slaves. They are recorded returns of sales of slaves and are filed according to the type of sale, for example of slaves alone; sales of slaves with land and buildings of estates; sales through judicial process of the Court of Chancery, or through the marshal's office.

NDO 4, West Indies Slave Compensation, 1835 to 1842, contains payment books which show the sum awarded, the date of the Treasury warrant, and contain the signatures of the claimants' representatives. There are also miscellaneous accounts, and correspondence, and some certificates of deaths and marriages.

Further reading:

Craton, Michael, 'Changing Patterns of Slave Families in the British West Indies', in *Journal of Interdisciplinary History*, vol 10, 1979, pp 1-35.

Gutman, Herbert, *The Black Family in Slavery and Freedom, 1750-1925* (Oxford, Basil Blackwell, 1976).

Higman, B W, *Slave Population and Economy in Jamaica, 1807-1834* (Cambridge University Press, 1976).

Rose, James, *Black Genesis* (Detroit, Gale Research Company, 1978).

Streets, David H, *Slave Genealogy: A Research Guide With Case Studies* (Maryland, Heritage Books Inc, 1986).

Young, Tommie Morton, *Afro-American Genealogy Source Book* (London, Garland Publishing, Inc, 1987).

Chapter 9: The Colonial Civil Servant

On 1 October 1930 the Personnel Division of the Colonial Office came into existence. Prior to 1930 the Secretary of State had entire control of the appointment of persons to all but the most subordinate official posts which were appointed by the governor. They were under his 'patronage' which was dealt with in his private office by his private secretaries. There were three classes of post, based on salary. Class 3 positions were the most subordinate and were appointed entirely by the governor. For class 2 posts the governor would make a provisional appointment which was reported to the Secretary of State for confirmation, and seldom refused. The governor could recommend class 1 officers, but on the understanding that the Secretary of State had the final decision. From 1930 there was a gradual unification of the various colonial posts, such as administration, forestry, agriculture, medicine and railways, and the selection of candidates under the control of the Secretary of State was not just by salary grade, but also by post.

From 1900 there were the rudiments of a centrally managed service. When senior posts in the colonies became vacant, officials of the Colonial Office would review the records and qualifications of officers already in the service and make recommendations to the Secretary of State for filling vacancies by promotion or transfer. Promotion to higher posts was frequently made by transfer from one colony to another. Claims of officers already serving were considered before any posts were filled by recruitment from outside, and promotion was based on official qualifications, experience and merit. The Secretary of State recruited and nominated candidates from outside to fill vacancies but could also offer a post in one territory to an officer already serving in another.

The records of the Patronage Department, 1867-1919, are in CO 429. The registers (CO 430) relate not only to the Patronage original correspondence, but to original correspondence records of individual colonies. Letters applying for specific appointment were registered in the colonial registers. In 1930 the Personnel Division was established. It was made up of an Appointments Department, dealing with recruitment and training, and a Colonial Service Department, concerned with promotions and transfers, conditions of employment and pensions. The records of the Personnel Division, 1932-1952,

WINDWARD ISLANDS—GRENADA.

Population.

Census, 1871	37,684.
Census, 1881	42,403.
Estimate, 1889	53,393.
Census, 1891	53,203.

Shipping Entered and Cleared.

Year.	Finances.		British Tonnage.	Total Tonnage.
	Revenue.	Expenditure.		
	£	£		
1881	37,176	39,396	169,297	175,305
1882	45,101	43,663	202,382	221,778
1883	43,883	46,976	226,992	237,340
1884	41,488	45,260	259,010	258,508
1885	41,894	44,103	245,418	250,327
1886	42,934	44,395	292,759	298,338
1887	46,743	44,804	276,661	282,977
1888	51,378	47,422	325,301	329,636
1889	56,441	51,086	332,052	338,107
1890	49,267	53,356	462,090	477,028

Customs revenue, 1890, 24,758*l.*

Imports.

Year.	From U.K.	From Colonies.	From Elsewhere.	Total.
	£	£	£	£
1881	80,043	39,003	12,939	131,985
1882	79,424	37,276	19,674	136,374
1883	69,391	47,472	18,402	135,265
1884	73,844	55,112	24,465	153,421
1885	63,324	56,141	18,639	138,105
1886	53,553	49,043	17,742	120,338
1887	73,366	47,786	22,093	143,185
1888	82,597	52,522	27,318	162,437
1889	87,761	45,733	40,587	174,081
1890	93,258	37,283	40,332	170,873

Exports.

Year.	To U.K.	To Colonies.	To Elsewhere.	Total.
	£	£	£	£
1881	180,604	11,647	2,028	194,279
1882	163,792	17,133	3,296	184,221
1883	155,737	11,836	25,951	193,524
1884	194,952	8,088	10,078	213,118
1885	158,901	9,866	9,953	178,720
1886	159,805	10,940	9,946	180,691
1887	185,216	10,612	22,121	217,949
1888	202,684	9,182	17,397	229,263
1889	172,912	7,514	15,169	195,595
1890	241,221	8,882	16,199	266,302

Public Debt, 1890, 63,391*l.*

Executive Council.

The Officer administering the Government.
The Colonial Secretary.
The Attorney-General.
The Treasurer.

P. Orgias, M.D., Colonial Surgeon
P. F. Macleod, M.D.
Charles Messervy, Director of Works.

Legislative Council.

The Officer administering the Government.
The Colonial Secretary.
The Attorney-General.

WINDWARD ISLANDS—GRENADA.

Unofficial Members, C. M. Browne, G. W. Williamson, F. Harford, W. S. Comissiong, Q.C., J. Patterson, D. Alexander, and F. Gurney, Esquires.
Clerk of the Councils, Marcus H. de la Poer Beresford, 150*l.*

Civil Establishment.

Governor-in-Chief, Windward Islands, The Hon. Sir Walter F. Hely-Hutchinson, K.C.M.G., 2,500*l.*
Private Secretary, C. F. Sitwell, 300*l.*
Chief Clerk in the Governor's Office, M. H. De la Poer Beresford (also Clerk of Councils), 150*l.*
Second Clerk, R. C. Grannum, 160*l.*
Colonial Secretary and Registrar-General, L. R. Fyfe, 500*l.*
Chief Clerk, Colonial Secretary's Office, C. H. Collymore, 250*l.*, and fees as District Registrar.
Assistant Clerk, E. M. Martin, 40*l.*
Treasurer and Manager of Savings' Bank, Edward Drayton, 500*l.* and fees.
Chief Clerk, Treasury, E. J. McEwen, 250*l.* (260*l.* personal), 100*l.*
Second ditto,
Assistant G. Smith, 40*l.*
Accountant, J. Harbin, 200*l.*

Revenue Officers :—
Chief Rev. Officer, J. G. Wells, 250*l.*, and 50*l.* allce.; A. Webster, 200*l.*, and fees as District Registrar; E. H. Moore, and 50*l.* for horse; J. H. Thomas, Moses Rapier, J. F. E. Roberts, S. W. M. Roche, 120*l.*, and 30*l.* for horse; W. E. Haynes, 220*l.*, and fees as District Registrar.
Carriacou, D. Ferguson, 200*l.*, boat, and fees as District Registrar.
Asst. Rev. Officer, G. E. Gumbs, 100*l.*
Postmaster, John Griffith, 250*l.*
Director of Public Works, C. Messervy, 650*l.*, 30*l.* house allowance, and 100*l.* allowance.
Clerk and Storekeeper, A. N. Comissiong, 100*l.* and 50*l.* from loan funds.
Assistant Clerk, J. A. Martin, 60*l.*

Medical Officers :—
Colonial Surgeon, P. Orgias, M.D., 400*l.* and allowance.
District No. 1, and Asylum, P. F. McLeod, M.D., 400*l.*, and quarters.
District No. 2, E. F. Hatton, M.B., M.R.C.S., 300*l.*
District No. 3, William Laing, M.D., 300*l.*
District No. 4, L. M. Enos, 300*l.*
District No. 5, G. L. Latour, M.D., M.R.C.S.E., 300*l.*

Colonial Surgeon, P. Orgias, M.D., 400*l.* and allowance.
District No. 1, and Asylum, P. F. McLeod, M.D., 400*l.*, and quarters.
*L. and L.M., K.Q.C.P.I., 300*l.**
Asst. Surgeon, Colony Hospital, W. Boyd, L.K.Q.C.P.I., L.R.C.S.I., 250*l.* and quarters.

Keeper of Immigration Records, C. H. Collymore, 50*l.*
Superintendent of Prisons, J. M. Lush, 225*l.*, and quarters.
Midwife, Female Prison, J. Fitt, 35*l.* and quarters.
Chief of Police and Sanitary Inspector, H. T. Wright, 300*l.*, 50*l.* allowance, and quarters.
Inspector of Schools, E. W. Begrie, 300*l.*, allowance 50*l.*
Librarian, J. Braithwaite, 75*l.*

WINDWARD ISLANDS—ST. LUCIA.

251

Judicial Establishment.

Chief Justice, Judge of the Vice-Admiralty Court, and Vice-Chancellor, J. F. Gresham, *Advocate,* H. R. Hamerton-General, and *Admrl* private practice.
Bar Schools, 400*l.*, with Supreme Court, and in Vice-Registrar of J. Falconer Anton, 300*l.*
Admiralty, ditto, and Marshal in Vice-Admiralty.
Chief Clerk, A. Martin, 150*l.*
Second ditto, G. A. Jackson, 80*l.*
Third ditto, G. G. Munro.
Police Magistrates and Coroners : Southern District, J. E. L. Sergeant, 400*l.*, and 125*l.* allowances.
Northern District, S. E. Roche, 300*l.*, and 25*l.* allowance.
Eastern District, J. P. G. Munro, 300*l.*, and 50*l.* allowance.
Western District, L. B. Otway, 300*l.*, and 50*l.* allowance.

Chief Ministers of Religion.

Anglican Church.

Bishop, The Bishop of Barbados (Dr. Bree).
Archdeacon, The Ven. H. Hutson.
Roman Catholic Church, Rev. de Martini.
Wesleyan, Rev. E. Donald Jones.
Presbyterian, Rev. James Rae.

ST. LUCIA.

Situation and Area.

The island of St. Lucia was discovered by Columbus, during his fourth voyage, on the 15th June, 1502. It is situated in 13° 50' N. lat., and 60° 58' W. long., at a distance of 24 miles to the south-east of Martinique, and 21 to the north-east of St. Vincent. It is 24 miles in length, and 12 at its greatest breadth; its circumference is 150 miles, and its area 243 sq. miles, rather less than Middlesex. Near its northern extremity lies Pigeon Island, formerly a military post of some importance. Castries, the capital of the island, contains about 1200 houses, and a population of over 6,000 souls. Next in importance is the town of Soufrière, containing a population of about 2,000 souls.

History.

At the period of its discovery, St. Lucia was inhabited by the Caribs, and continued in their possession till 1635, when it was granted by the King of France to MM. de L'Olive and Duplessis. In 1639 the English formed their first settlement, but in the following year the colonists were all murdered by the Caribs. In 1642 the King of France, still claiming a right of sovereignty over the island, ceded it to the French West India Company, who in 1650 sold it for 1,660*l.* to MM. Houel and Du Parquet. After frequent attempts by the Caribs to expel the French, the latter concluded a Treaty of Peace with them in 1660. In 1663, Thomas Warner, the natural son of the Governor of St. Christopher, made a descent on St. Lucia. The English continued in possession till the Peace of Breda in 1667, when the island was restored to the Crown of France; and in 1674 it was re-annexed to the Crown of France, and made a dependency of Martinique. After the Peace of Utrecht, in 1713, the rival pretensions of England and France to the posses-

---

sion of St. Lucia resulted in open hostility. In 1718 the Regent d'Orléans made a grant of the island to Marshal d'Estrées, and in 1722 the King of England made a following year, however, a body of troops, despatched to St. Lucia by the Governor of Martinique, compelled the English settlers to evacuate the island, and it was declared neutral.

In 1744, the French took advantage of the declaration of war to resume possession of St. Lucia, which they retained till the Treaty of Aix-la-Chapelle in 1748, when it was again declared neutral. In 1756, on the renewal of hostilities, the French put the island in a state of defence; but in 1762 it surrendered to the joint operations of Admiral Rodney and General Monckton. In the following year, by the Treaty of Paris, it was assigned to France.

St. Lucia continued in the peaceable possession of the French till 1778, when effective measures were taken by the British for its conquest. In the early part of 1782, Rodney took up his station in Gros Islet Bay, with a fleet of 36 sail of the line, and it was from thence that he pursued Comte de Grasse, whom he gained the memorable battle of the 12th April in that year. This event was followed by the Peace of Versailles, and St. Lucia was once more restored to France.

In 1794, on the declaration of war against revolutionary France, the West Indies became the scene of a series of naval and military operations which resulted in the surrender of St. Lucia to the British arms, on the 4th of April, 1794.

In 1796 the British Government despatched to the relief of their West Indian possessions a body of troops, 12,000 strong, under the command of Sir Ralph Abercrombie, supported by a squadron under Admiral Sir Hugh Christian. On the 26th April these forces appeared off St. Lucia, and after an obstinate and sanguinary contest, which lasted till the 26th May, the Republican party, which had been aided by insurgent slaves under Victor Hughes, laid down their arms, and surrendered as prisoners of war.

By the British retained possession of St. Lucia till 1802, when it was restored to France by the Treaty of Amiens; but on the renewal of hostilities it surrendered by capitulation to General Greenfield on the 22nd June, 1803, since which period it has continued under British rule.

General Description.

On its final acquisition by the English, the island had become much depopulated, partly by war, but chiefly by intestine struggles, the fruits of the French Revolution. The recovery from this state of things has been slow, having been retarded by the severe epidemics of cholera and small-pox which have at different times visited the West Indies. Each census, however, has shown an advance in this respect, and the population now amounts to about 42,220. Most of the inhabitants speak a French patois, but English is gradually becoming general. The population is gradually receding, of European descent, the remainder being of the negro race, except about 2,050 East Indian immigrants. The reputation of the island for peculiar unhealthiness is undeserved. The average death-rate for the last years, though lower than that of some other islands situated in the valleys between high mountains are undoubtedly unhealthy, but are becoming less and less so as the forests fall before a yearly extending cultivation. The danger from venomous reptiles is also much

---

250

Figure 19   *Colonial Office List 1892, p 250*: list of Grenada officials, and history of St Lucia.

DOMINIONS OFFICE AND COLONIAL OFFICE LIST.

684

Barbados, W.I., to Aug., 1897; asst. auditor, Sierra Leone and Gambia, Sept., 1897, to Jan., 1900; acted auditor May to Nov., 1898; asst. auditor, Gold Coast and Lagos, Jan. to Mar, 1900; auditor, March, 1900; introduced system double entry accounts Gold Coast P.O., July, 1901; prepared scheme for introduction of double entry system of accounts for Accra town council, Aug., 1901; local auditor. Cyprus, 1902; auditor-gen., Mauritius, Apr., 1909; recvr.-gen., Mauritius, 1912; ag.col. sec., on various occasions, 1919–20 and 1922-23; col. sec., Aug., 1923; admstd. govt. on various occasions, 1924-30; ret., 1931.

GRANNUM, REGINALD CLIFTON, C.M.G. (1925). —B. 1872; 2nd clk. to gov., Windward Is., Sept., 1891; ditto, St. Vincent, Apr., 1892; supvr. of cust., G. Coast Col., Oct., 1893; asst. local audr., G. Coast and Lagos, May, 1895; local audr., S. Leone, June 1896; J.P., S. Leone, 1897; ch. asst. treas., G. Coast, Apr., 1903; ag. treas. and mem. ex. and leg. couns., mem. bd. of educ., July, 1903, to June, 1904, Dec., 1904, to Dec., 1905, June, 1906, to May, 1907; Oct., 1907, to Sept., 1908; admitted student of Gray's Inn, Aug., 1908; recvr.-gen., B. Guiana, Sept., 1908; mem. of exec. and legis. couns., Dec., 1908; ag. govt. sec., July to Oct., 1913; deputy gov., Sept. to Oct., 1913; treas. and mem., exec. and leg. couns., Kenya, Sept., 1922.

GRANT, D. K. S.—Asst. conservator of forests E.A.P., Dec., 1912; conservator of forests, Tanganyika Territory, Dec., 1920.

GRANT, EZEKIEL AUGUSTUS. — Ent. British Honduras civ. serv. after compet. exam., as copyist to survey dept., Nov., 1899; 3rd cls. clk. (asst. keeper), King's warehouse, Feb., 1906; 2nd cls. clk., P.W.D., Apr., 1907; on active serv. with B.W.I. Regt. during war, Apr., 1916 to July, 1919; ag. 1st cls. clk., P.W.D., Aug., 1919 to Mar., 1920; acct., P.W.D., Apr., 1920; ag. ch. clk. and storekeeper, P.W.D., Apr., 1921; ag. asst. inspr., schls., during 1921 to 1923; asst. inspr., schls., provisionally, Apr., 1923; barrister-at-law, Inner Temple, 1928; dist. comsnr., Orange Walk, Nov., 1928; ag. atty.-gen., Apr. to May, 1931; ag. dist. comsnr., Belize and offl. admstr. and offl. recr. from Apr., 1931.

GRANT, LIONEL KEITH.—B. 1875; ent. civ. serv., Barbados, 1894; ch.clk. P.O., 1913; acctnt., 1926; ag. col. postmr. various periods, 1927-30; ch. clk., audit office, 1931; audr.-gen., 1934.

GRANT, PETER.— B. 1883; Hong Kong pol., Nov., 1906; inspr., ditto, Dec., 1923; ch., ditto, Mar., 1928; King's pol. med., 1933; asst. supt., pol., Feb., 1933.

GRANT, RICHARD WILLIAM, M.C.—B. 1897; ed. Jones' Schl., Mon. and Royal Mil. Acad., Woolwich; cadet, S.S., Nov., 1920; attd., col. secs'. office, Dec., 1920; offr., cls V, dist. offr., N. Tebal, Nov., 1923; offr., cls. IV, Nov., 1927; dist. offr., Bentong, Dec., 1929; asst. advr., K. Tinggi, Mar., 1930; offr., cls. III, Nov., 1932; asst. advr., Segamat, Oct., 1933; ag. 1st asst. sec. (A), S.S., Feb., 1935.

GRANTHAM, ALEXANDER WILLIAM GEORGE HERDER, M.A. (Cantab.), Barrister-at-Law.—B. 1899; cadet, Hong-Kong, Nov., 1922; attd., C.S.O., 1925; 2nd pol. mag., Sept., 1929; sec. retrenchment comtee., July, 1930; asst. to P.M.G. in addn., July, 1930; dist. offr., South, in addn., Dec., 1930; extra asst. col. sec., and sec. to harbr. advisory comtee., 1931; 1st pol. mag. in addn., 1932; 2nd asst. col. sec. and dep. clk. of couns., June, 1933; extra asst. col. sec., Apr., 1935; col. sec., Bermuda, 1935.

GRANTHAM, SIDNEY HOWARD.—B. 1883; clk., W.O., Apr., 1901; asst. acct., army accts. dept., Apr., 1904; served S. Africa, 1904-07 and 1912-14; asst. commr., pol., Nigeria, May, 1915; senr. ditto, Apr., 1930; asst. inspr.-gen., pol., Jan., 1931; ag. inspr.-gen., pol., in 1932, 1933 and 1934; dep. inspr.-gen., pol., July, 1934.

GRAVER, GEORGE STANLEY, A.M.I.C.E.—B. 1898; ed. Devonport High Schl.; engnr., P.W.D., Hong Kong, 1923; ag. exec. engnr., May-Dec., 1933.

GRAY, CHAS. EDGAR.—B. 1904; cler. asst., offl. recr's. office, Br. Guiana, 1919; 6th cls. offr., col. sec's. office, 1921; 5th cls. offr., 1923; 4th cls. offr., 1926; sec. to prisons comtee., 1928; 2nd cls. clk., 1933; ag. prin. clk. and clk., exec. and leg. couns. in 1932 and 1933.

GRAY, H. W., O.B.E.—Office supt., lieut. gov.'s off., E.A.P., May, 1908; clk. of the couns., Oct., 1908; asst. dist. comsnr., 1911; dist. comsnr., Kenya, Jan., 1920; ch. regisr. of natives, Jan., 1920.

GRAY, JOHN, B.A., M.D., M.B., B.Ch., B.A.O. (Dub.), L.M., Rot. Hosp. (Dub.), certif. L.S.T.M.—B. 1882; med. offr., gen. hosp., Singapore, Apr., 1909; grade II, F.M.S., Apr., 1910; sr. surgn., class III, Oct., 1913; ch. med. offr., Malacca, Jan., 1919; ch. med. offr., Singapore, Nov., 1920; ag. prin. civil med. offr., S.S., and tempy. M.L.C., for various periods, 1923-31; state surgn., Kedah, Oct., 1931.

GRAY, JOHN MACFARLANE, L.R.C.P., L.K.C.S. (I), L.M. (Rot), D.P.H. (Univ. Dub.).—B. 1898; health offr., med. dept., Hong Kong, 1933; ag. M.O.H., 1934.

GRAY, JOHN MILNER.—B. 1889; ed. Perse Schl. and King's Coll., Cambridge, M.A.; admitted solr., sup. ct., 1923; called to bar, Gray's Inn, Apr., 1932; war serv. with B.E.F., France (twice wounded); asst. dist. comsnr., Uganda Prot., 1920; mag., 1924; ag. solr.-gen., 1929; ag. puisne judge, 1933; judge, sup. ct, Gambia, 1934; O.A.G., May, 1935.

GRAY, R.—B. 1880; clk., treasy., 1902; clk., rev. dept., 1904; dep. recr., rev., Lichtenburg, 1905; clk., rev. dept., Jo'burg, 1908; Pretoria, 1912; prin. clk., 1921; survr., 1928; acctnt., 1929; recr., rev., E. London, 1931; do., Pretoria, 1932; do., Durban, 1933.

GRAY, SIR REGINALD, KT. BACH. (1920), K.C. (1908).—B. 1851; called to the bar, Inner Tem., 1875; compiled, in 1884, Bermuda laws from 1690-1883; revising offr., Bermuda, 1889-93; compiled, in 1903, Bermuda laws from 1690-1902; counsel to statute law consolidation comtee. since 1900; atty.-gen., Bermuda, 28th May, 1900; ag. chief just. in Oct. and Nov., 1911; ex-officio mem. of exec. coun.; M.L.A., 1895-1897, 1900-1906, and from 1907; ret.

GRAY. THEODORE GRANT, M.B., Ch.B. (Aberdeen), M.P.C.—B. 1884; ed. Aberdeen Grammar Schl. and Aberdeen Univ.; asst. med. offr., 1911; med. supt., Nelson (N.Z.) mental hosp., 1920; med. supt., Auckland mental hosp., 1924; dep. inspr.gen. mental hosps., N.Z., 1925; inspr.-gen., 1927.

GRAY, MAJOR WILLIAM BAIN, C.B.E. (1935). —B. 1886; ed. George Watson's Coll., Edinburgh; Univ. of Edinburgh; M.A., 1st cls. hons., Gladstone Prize and Ph.D., and New Coll., Oxford, B.Litt.; some time Carnegie Research Fellow; lect., Tech. Coll., Brighton examnr., Univ. of Edinburgh, Oxford and Cambridge joint bd. and Oxford local exams.

Figure 20   *Colonial Office List 1936, p 684*: page showing career of R C Grannum, one of the author's forebears.

St Vincent
~~GRENADA.~~

APPLICATION for Employment in the Government Service.

FORM to be filled up by the Applicant himself and returned to the Colonial Secretary.

C. O.
13682

Rec^d
22 SEP 92

...full........	Reginald Clifton Grannum
...Application........	6th September 1892
...n or occupation........	Second Clerk Government Office
....	Kingstown St Vincent
...Name........	Edward Thomas Grannum
...n or occupation........	Public Accountant
....	Bridgetown Barbados.

...his Name and Profession nevertheless be given.

...year of birth........	17th April 1872 Age last birthday 20
...birth........	Barbados
...single, married, or a widower,	Single
...of children, Sons........	—— Aged respectively ——
...Daughters........	—— " " ——

...cation—
...the Schools or Colleges at you received your education, ...sional as well as general; ...ce in each case the date of ...and leaving........

Harrison College Barbados entered in 1881 left early in 1888.
Ontario Business College – Belleville Ont. Canada entered 17th May 1889 – graduated 24th October 1889
Copy of Diploma attached

...onal qualifications (if any,) ...e date at which each was ob-

...ment from completion of edu-
...to present time........

Served Messrs Grannum Street Public Accountants Barbados from April 1888 to April 1889 left drew to go to Canada – served for a short period with Messrs I. F. & F. H. Harrington – Commission Merchants, Belleville Ont, Canada – left drew to return to the West Indies Served in Governor's Office, Grenada, as Second Clerk from 29th April 1891 to 21st April 1892.
I am now receiving £100 per annum.

...each position held by you, ...ates between which you held ...d the cause of leaving; and ...salary you are now receiving

...tment desired........
...do not apply for a particular ...intment you should state what ...e lowest salary that you would ...t..

any appointment with a salary of not less than £200 per annum, and free quarters, in any part of West Africa – Sierra Leone preferred.

[Turn over.]

72

Figure 21   Application form of R C Grannum, dated 10 September 1892.
(CO 321/143)

are in CO 850 with the registers in CO 919. Those of the Appointments Department together with some earlier correspondence, 1920-1952, are in CO 877 with the registers in CO 918. In 1945 the division was renamed the Colonial Service Division, and was changed again to the Overseas Service Division in 1954. The records of the Colonial Service Division and Overseas Service Division, 1948-1962, are in CO 1017.

There is no one series of records to trace the career of colonial officials. The commissions of most senior colonial officers, such as governor, chief justice, chief auditor, naval officer, and councillors were recorded in the Privy Council registers (PC 2 and PC 5), letters patent (C 66), and in the Colonial entry books (CO 324). The appointment was also announced in the *London Gazette* (ZJ 1) and in colonial gazettes. Colonial appointments by the Secretary of State, 1819-1835, are in CO 323.

From 1862 the first place to look for colonial civil servants is the annual *Colonial Office List*, available in the Reference Room, which lists all officers employed by colonial governments. This periodical briefly describes the history and economy of each colony, and lists government employees with their salaries. At the back of each volume there are potted biographies of senior colonial officials.

The original correspondence classes contain the governors' recommendations of appointment, promotion and transfer. They also include individuals' letters to the Secretary of State asking for appointment. Other records to be found include application forms, medical reports, and applications for leave, half pay, retirement, and pension. The Blue Books of Statistics list government employees and government pensioners. Government gazettes give notification of appointment, promotion, and transfer of officials, and leave of absence and resumption of duty.

Further reading:

Bertram, Sir Anton, *The Colonial Service* (Cambridge, Cambridge University Press, 1930).

Colonial Office List, annual publication 1862-

Fiddes, Sir George, *The Dominions and Colonial Offices* (London, G P Putnam's Sons Ltd, 1926).

Jeffries, Charles, *The Colonial Empire and its Civil Service* (Cambridge University Press, 1938).

Jeffries, Charles, *Whitehall and the Colonial Service: An Administrative Memoir, 1939-1956* (London, The Athlone Press, 1972).

Chapter 10: Emigration to the United Kingdom

Since the settling of the West Indies, West Indians have returned or emigrated to Britain. Many planters and merchants sent their children to school in England. Many retired to Britain, and brought their servants, including slaves, with them. West Indian merchant seamen were discharged and settled in the seaports of Glasgow, Cardiff and Liverpool. The records of these immigrants are to be found among the usual sources one would use to trace British ancestors, such as wills, the decennial censuses, and parish records. The British government has not registered people entering these shores and there are no comprehensive lists of West Indian immigrants. British West Indians were British subjects and did not need to naturalize when they emigrated to Britain. The only lists of immigrants from the West Indies are the inwards passenger lists in BT 26 which cover the period 1878 to 1960. These lists contain the names of persons arriving in British ports and are arranged by the year and month of arrival, the port of arrival and the name of ship. The information given includes name, age, occupation, and address in the United Kingdom. It is important to note that these passenger lists are only for ships landing in Britain. Information received by the Ministry of Labour from the Colonial Office relating to West Indians arriving in 1955 (LAB 26/1902) shows that many arrived by train to London Victoria, via Calais and Dover, after disembarking from their ships at Continental ports such as Marseilles, Genoa, and Vigo. The PRO does not hold these passenger lists. There are no records of passengers who travelled by aeroplane.

It was not until this century, and more especially since the Second World War, that large numbers of West Indians arrived in Britain. It might be useful to describe some of the more recent immigration by West Indians. During the First World War many West Indians served as merchant seamen and settled down in the seaports familiar to them such as Glasgow, Cardiff, Liverpool, and London. On the outbreak of the Second World War many West Indians were recruited for war service in the United Kingdom, and many stayed when the war ended. 1200 British Hondurians were recruited to fell timber in Scotland, and about 500 remained; 10,000 West Indians, in particular Jamaicans, were recruited as ground crews in the Royal Air Force (RAF), about 2000 remained; and many who served in the merchant navy remained. After the war many of those who served in the RAF used their gratuities to pay for passages

BT 26/1237/London, June 1948

25 JUN 1948 3624

P.M. 22

Wt.33481/028 30,000 4/46 W.H.&S. 444/41

Merchant Shipping Act, 1906, and Aliens Restriction Acts, 1914 and 1919.

IN-COMING PASSENGERS

Returns of Passengers brought to the United Kingdom in ships arriving from Places out of Europe, and not within the Mediterranean Sea.

NOTES (a)—All Passengers brought by such ships are to be included, whether arriving from European or from non-European ports. 1st Class, 2nd Class, Tourist Class, and 3rd Class Passengers are to be entered in separate groups.

(b)—In the case of those ships which are engaged in pleasure cruises starting and ending in the United Kingdom the full particulars required by this form should only be furnished in respect of those passengers who embark at a port abroad and disembark in the United Kingdom.

Ship's Name	Official Number	Steamship Line	Registered Tonnage	Master's Name	Voyage
M.V. "EMPIRE WINDRUSH"	181561.	THE NEW ZEALAND SHIPPING CO,LTD., 138,LEADENHALL STREET, LONDON.E.C.3.	14414.24.	JOHN G.ALMOND.	TRINIDAD, KINGSTON, From TAMPICO, HAVANA, BERMUDA. To Tilbury

Date of Arrival 21. 6. 1948.

NAMES AND DESCRIPTIONS OF BRITISH PASSENGERS

(1) Port of Embarkation	(2) Port at which Passengers have been landed	(3) NAMES OF PASSENGERS	(4) CLASS (Whether 1st, 2nd, Tourist or 3rd)	(5) AGES OF PASSENGERS — Adults of 12 years and upwards, Accompanied by husband or wife Males	Females	Not Accompanied by husband or wife Males	Females	Children between 1 and 12 Males	Females	Infants Males	Females	(6) Proposed Address in the United Kingdom	(7) Profession Occupation or Calling of Passengers	(8) Country of last Permanent Residence*	(9) Country of Intended Future Permanent Residence* — England	Wales	Scotland	Northern Ireland	Eire	Other parts of the British Empire	Foreign Countries
TRINIDAD.	Tilbury	AUSTIN Richard	"A"		48							113,Boleyn Rd,Forest Gate,London.E.7.	Marine Engineer.	England.	*						
"	"	ARMSTRONG Grace	"		35							24,Scotland Rd,Carlisle.	Missionary.	Trinidad.							*
"	"	BALL Felicity	"		24							Kingsmill,Bucks.	H.D.	"							*
"	"	" Michael	"					2				- do -		"							*
"	"	BRITTEN Percy	"	47								Cortina,Blenheim Rd, Bickley.	Master Mariner.	England.	*						
"	"	BARROW Lucy	"		19							45,Manor Lane, Lewisham,S.E.13.	Student.	Trinidad.							*
"	"	BAPTISITE Mona	"		21							3,Pewyern Rd, London,S.W.5.	Clerk.	"							*
"	"	BALLANTYNE Gordon	"	28								52,Boardmans Lane, St.Helens,Lancs.	Planter.	Br.Guiana.	*						
"	"	" Maria	"		31							- do -	H.D.	"							*
"	"	" Gordon	"									- do -	-	"							*
"	"	BAILEY McDonald	"		67							4,Gt.James St, London.W.C.1,	Merchant.	Trinidad.	*						
"	"	CLARKE Ellis	"		30							50,Elm Park Gdns, Chelsea.S.W.10.	Barrister.	"							*
"	"	" Elma	"		57							- do -	H.D.	"							*
"	"	CHEN Gerald	"		36							33,Chatsworth Rd, London,N.W.2.	Civil Servant.	"							*
"	"	CUNARD Nancy	"		52							Patenhall,Bedford.	Writer.	France.							*
"	"	CHAPPLE Arthur	"	55								125,Erlanger Rd, New Cross,S.E.	Engineer.	Br.Guiana.	*						
"	"	" Bertha	"		52							- do -	H.D.	"	*						
"	"	DOMINIQUE Patrick.	"	40								c/o Colonial Office, London,W.1,	Civil Servant.	Trinidad.							*
"	"	" Marie	"		40							- do -	H.D.	"							*
"	"	DAVID Daniel	"	39								113,Boultham Park Rd, Lincoln.	Customs Officer.	"							*
"	"	DICK James	"				22					Fair Orchard Farm, St.Bridew,Nr.Newport.	Student.	England.							*
"	"	" Rita	"		28							113,Boultham Park Rd, Lincoln.	H.D.	Trinidad.							*
"	"	" Heather	"								1½	- do -		"							*

*By Permanent Residence is to be understood residence for a year or more. Northern Ireland and Eire are to be regarded as separate countries.

[OVER

C. 439

Sec. 02771/1945

Figure 22   Passenger list of the *Empire Windrush*, June 1948. (BT 26/1237)

back to Britain. The PRO does not hold the records of those recruited for war service. The records of those who served in the armed forces are still held by the Ministry of Defence; and the records of merchant seamen are held by the Registrar General of Shipping and Seamen. During the 1960s British Rail and London Transport recruited many West Indians: these schemes appear to have been conducted in the West Indies and there are few records in the PRO.

Many papers reflecting the concerns of Parliament and government departments about coloured immigrant labourers are to be found among the records of the Cabinet Office, the Home Office, the Colonial Office, and the Ministry of Labour. An information sheet listing sources in the Public Record Office on post-war West Indian immigration and labour is available from the Reference Room, Kew.

British West Indians have not only emigrated to the United Kingdom, many have left their islands for other West Indian islands, the United States, Canada and Australia. The Public Record Office does not hold any records of these emigrants unless the ship after leaving a British port picked up passengers in the West Indies en route to America, etc.

Further reading:

PRO Records Information Leaflets

70 - *Immigration*

Diamond, Ian, and Clarke, Sue, 'Demographic Patterns Among Britain's Ethnic Groups', in *The Changing Population of Britain*, ed Heather Joshi (Oxford, Basil Blackwell, 1989), pp 177-198.

Fryer, Peter, *Staying Power. The History of Black People in Britain* (London, Pluto Press, 1984).

Layton-Henry, Zig, *The Politics of Immigration. Immigration, Race and Race Relations in Post-war Britain* (Oxford, Blackwell, 1992).

Shyllon, Folarin, *Black people in Britain 1555-1833* (Oxford University Press, 1977).

Walvin, James, *Black and White. The Negro and English Society 1555-1945* (London, Penguin Press, 1973).

Chapter 11: Non-British Colonies

Most of the records of British subjects on non-British West Indian islands are to be found in the records of the Foreign Office. These are predominantly official despatches between Britain's representatives abroad and the Foreign Office. The records are arranged by country. However, before independence this was the colonial power. For example, records of St Thomas will be found under Denmark, and those for St Eustatius are under Holland and the Netherlands.

There are three types of archives:

General correspondence. Papers created and accumulated in the Foreign Office and are composed of originals of despatches from British officials abroad, and drafts of outgoing correspondence. Until 1906 these are arranged by country. From 1906 general correspondence for all countries are filed in subject classes.

Embassy and consular archives. Papers created by the embassies. These are original correspondence received from the Foreign Office, local correspondence from other embassies and consulates, and with the government of the foreign state. These records include wills, naturalizations, passport registers, and papers of the disposal of estates. For example FO 986 the embassy and consular archives for Panama City includes many records on the estates of British West Indians, many of whom are named in the class list.

Consular archives. These are mainly registers held by the consul, such as registers of births, marriages and deaths of British subjects, and passport registers. Under the Consular Marriages Act 1848, consular staff were to maintain a marriage register of British subjects and to send returns to the Registrar General in London. Where staff were informed of births and deaths these were also returned to London. These consular returns are held by the Registrar General's Office, St Catherine's House, Kingsway, London WC8 6JP.

Before 1782 the records of foreign affairs are to be found among the State Papers Foreign (SP) classes.

The PRO also holds miscellaneous foreign returns of births, marriages and deaths for 1826 to 1951 which were originally deposited at the Registrar General's Office. These returns are in RG 32-RG 35, and are indexed in RG 43.

Many West Indian islands of other European powers were at times occupied and administered by Britain. Surinam was originally a British settlement. In Santo Domingo British forces joined with the French forces during the slave uprising from 1793, until both countries evacuated in 1803. Most islands, however, were invaded and administered by British forces during periods of war. During the Seven Years War, 1756-1763, Guadeloupe (1759-1763), Martinique (1762-1763), and Havana (1762-1763) were occupied. During the French Revolutionary and Napoleonic Wars, 1793-1815, Curaçao (1800-1802, 1807-1814), Guadeloupe (1810-1813), Martinique (1794-1815), St Croix (1810-1815), St Eustatius (1807-1815), St Thomas (1807-1815), and Surinam (1799-1802, 1804-1816), were occupied.

Records during these periods of occupation are to be found among the records of the War Office, Colonial Office, and the Treasury. Information recorded includes censuses, lists of government officials, and plantation returns; identified references are in section 5.2.1 and Appendix 2. During periods of occupation foreign troops were often taken into British service. The means of reference to the War Office records is through Public Record Office Lists and Indexes, vol LIII, *An Alphabetical Guide to certain War Office and other Military Records*.

Records of non-British West Indian islands

Cuba
before 1898 *see* Spain

General Correspondence	1901-1905	FO 108
Embassy and Consular archives	1870-1957	FO 277

Denmark
includes **St Thomas** and **St Croix**

State Papers Foreign	1577-1780	SP 75
General Correspondence	1781-1905	FO 22
Embassy and Consular archives	1781-1957	FO 211

    St Croix

Correspondence etc	1808-1815	CO 244, WO 1

    St Thomas

Correspondence etc	1808-1815	CO 259, WO 1

Dominican Republic (*formerly* **Santo Domingo**)
before 1821 *see* Spain
1822-1844 *see* Haiti

Correspondence etc	1693-1805	CO 245, WO 1

Santo Domingo
Claims Committee	1794-1812	T 81
General Correspondence	1848-1905	FO 23
Embassy and Consular archives	1848-1948	FO 140
Cuidad Trujillo consular archives	1811-1932	FO 68

France
includes **Martinique** and **Guadeloupe**
State Papers	1577-1780	SP 78
General Correspondence	1781-1905	FO 27
Embassy and Consular archives	1814-1957	FO 146

Martinique
Correspondence etc	1693-1815	CO 166, WO 1

Haiti
before 1824 *see* France
General Correspondence	1825-1905	FO 35
Embassy and Consular archives	1833-1947	FO 866
Aux Cayes consular archives	1870-1907	FO 376

Holland and the **Netherlands**
includes **Curaçao, St Eustatius** and **Surinam**
State Papers	c.1560-1780	SP 84
General Correspondence	1781-1905	FO 37
Embassy and Consular archives	1811-1956	FO 238
Netherlands Antilles consular archives		FO 907
Miscellanea	1815-1908	FO 241

Curaçao
Correspondence etc	1800-1816	CO 66, WO 1

St Eustatius
Correspondence etc	1779-1783	CO 246

Surinam
Correspondence etc	1667-1832	CO 278, CO 111, WO 1
Surinam Absentees Sequestered Property Commission	1813-1822	T 75

Spain
includes **Cuba, Puerto Rico** and **Manila**
State Papers	1577-1780	SP 94
General Correspondence	1781-1905	FO 72
Embassy and Consular archives	1783-1962	FO 185

From 1906 Foreign Office general correspondence is filed in subject classes. There is a card index for 1906-1919, and a printed index 1920-1951. These are available in the Reference Room. The indexes to general correspondence, 1920-1951, have been published by Kraus International Publications in 131 volumes.

FO 371, Foreign Office political departments, is the main series of diplomatic correspondence. Other classes include FO 369, consular departments, which contains references to the protection and welfare of British subjects abroad such as the disposal of estates and wills, and FO 372, treaty departments, which includes papers on naturalization, extradition and passports.

Further reading:

PRO Records Information leaflets
no 22 - *Records of the Foreign Office from 1782*

Atherton, Louise, *'Never Complain, Never Explain'. Records of the Foreign Office and State Paper Office, 1500-c. 1960*, PRO Reader's Guide no 7 (London, PRO Publications, 1994).
Public Record Office Handbook no 13, *The records of the Foreign Office, 1782-1939* (London, HMSO, 1969).
Public Record Office Lists and Indexes, vol LIII, *An Alphabetical Guide to certain War Office and other Military Records preserved in the Public Record Office* (London, HMSO, 1931).
Lucas, C P, *Historical Geography of the British Colonies, Volume 2, the West Indies* (Oxford, Clarendon Press, 1890).

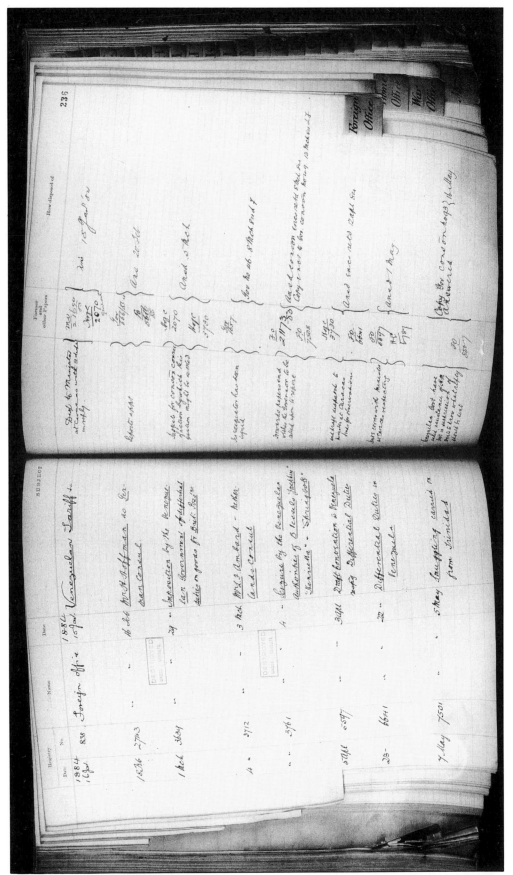

Figure 23   Page from Register of Correspondence for Trinidad, 1885. (CO 372/10)

81

Appendix 1: Colonial Office Classes

Colonies General

Colonial Papers	1574-1757	CO 1
Original Correspondence	1689-1952	CO 323
	1950-1960	CO 1032
Registers of Correspondence	1852-1952	CO 378
Registers of Out-letters	1871-1925	CO 379

Registry

General Registers	1623-1849	CO 326
Indexes to correspondence	1795-1874	CO 714
Daily Registers	1849-1929	CO 382

Antigua

Original Correspondence	1702-1872	CO 7
Registers of Correspondence	1850-1951	CO 354
Sessional Papers	1704-1966	CO 9
Government Gazettes	1872-1965	CO 156
	1967-1989	CO 1049
Miscellanea	1666-1887	CO 10
	1683-1945	CO 157
Registers of Out-letters	1872-1926	CO 507

Bahamas

Original Correspondence	1696-1951	CO 23
Registers of Correspondence	1850-1951	CO 333
Sessional Papers	1721-1965	CO 26
Government Gazettes	1894-1965	CO 564
Miscellanea	1721-1941	CO 27
Registers of Out-letters	1872-1926	CO 508

Barbados

Original Correspondence	1689-1951	CO 28
Registers of Correspondence	1850-1885	CO 376
	1886-1948	CO 565
Sessional Papers	1660-1965	CO 31

Government Gazettes	1867-1975	CO 32
Miscellanea	1678-1947	CO 33
Registers of Out-letters	1872-1926	CO 501

Bay Islands *(annexed by the Republic of Honduras in 1859)*

Original Correspondence	1852-1861	CO 34
Miscellanea	1855-1859	CO 36

Belize *(formerly British Honduras)*

Original Correspondence	1744-1951	CO 123
Registers of Correspondence	1855-1951	CO 348
Sessional Papers	1848-1965	CO 126
Government Gazettes	1861-1975	CO 127
Miscellanea	1807-1943	CO 128
Registers of Out-letters	1872-1926	CO 503

Bermuda

Original Correspondence	1689-1951	CO 37
Registers of Correspondence	1850-1951	CO 334
Sessional Papers	1687-1965	CO 40
Government Gazettes	1902-1965	CO 647
Miscellanea	1715-1950	CO 41
Registers of Out-letters	1872-1925	CO 499

Cayman Islands
see also under Jamaica

Sessional Papers	1908-1965	CO 857
Government Gazettes	1956-1990	CO 1019
Miscellanea	1912-1947	CO 651

Dominica

Original Correspondence	1730-1872	CO 71
	1872-1951	CO 152
Registers of Correspondence	1850-1951	CO 354
Sessional Papers	1767-1965	CO 74
Government Gazettes	1865-1975	CO 75

| Miscellanea | 1763-1940 | CO 76 |
| Registers of Out-letters | 1872-1926 | CO 507 |

Grenada

Original Correspondence	1747-1873	CO 101
	1874-1951	CO 321
Registers of Correspondence	1850-1951	CO 376
Sessional Papers	1777-1965	CO 104
Government Gazettes	1834-1975	CO 105
Miscellanea	1764-1938	CO 106
Registers of Out-letters	1872-1882	CO 504
	1883-1926	CO 377

Guyana (*formerly* British Guiana)

Original Correspondence	1781-1951	CO 111
Registers of Correspondence	1850-1951	CO 345
Sessional Papers	1805-1965	CO 114
Government Gazettes	1838-1965	CO 115
Miscellanea	1681-1943	CO 116
Registers of Out-letters	1872-1926	CO 502

Jamaica

Original Correspondence	1689-1951	CO 137
Registers of Correspondence	1850-1951	CO 351
Sessional Papers	1661-1965	CO 140
Government Gazettes	1794-1968	CO 141
Miscellanea	1658-1945	CO 142
Registers of Out-letters	1872-1926	CO 494

Leeward Islands

Original Correspondence	1689-1951	CO 152
Registers of Correspondence	1850-1951	CO 354
Sessional Papers	1680-1956	CO 155
Government Gazettes	1872-1965	CO 156
Miscellanea	1683-1945	CO 157
Registers of Out-letters	1872-1926	CO 507

Montserrat

Original Correspondence	1702-1872	CO 7
	1726-1872	CO 175
	1872-1951	CO 152
Registers of Correspondence	1850-1951	CO 354
Sessional Papers	1704-1965	CO 177
Miscellanea	1666-1829	CO 10
	1829-1887	CO 178
	1683-1945	CO 157
Registers of Out-letters	1872-1926	CO 507

Nevis

see also **St Christopher**

Original Correspondence	1689-1951	CO 152
	1703-1872	CO 184
	1816-1853	CO 239
Registers of Correspondence	1850-1951	CO 354
Sessional Papers	1721-1882	CO 186
Miscellanea	1704-1882	CO 187
Registers of Out-letters	1872-1926	CO 507

St Christopher

Original Correspondence	1689-1951	CO 152
	1702-1872	CO 239
Registers of Correspondence	1850-1951	CO 354
Sessional Papers	1704-1960	CO 241
Government Gazettes	1879-1989	CO 242
Miscellanea	1704-1887	CO 243
	1683-1945	CO 157
Registers of Out-letters	1872-1926	CO 507

St Lucia

Original Correspondence	1709-1783	CO 253
	1874-1951	CO 321
Registers of Correspondence	1850-1881	CO 367
	1882-1951	CO 376
Sessional Papers	1820-1965	CO 256
Government Gazettes	1857-1975	CO 257

Miscellanea	1722-1940	CO 258
Registers of Out-letters	1872-1882	CO 505
	1883-1926	CO 377

St Vincent

Original Correspondence	1668-1873	CO 260
	1874-1951	CO 321
Registers of Correspondence	1850-1951	CO 376
Sessional Papers	1769-1965	CO 263
Government Gazettes	1831-1975	CO 264
Miscellanea	1763-1941	CO 265
Registers of Out-letters	1872-1882	CO 506
	1883-1926	CO 377

Sierra Leone

Original Correspondence	1664-1951	CO 267
Registers of Correspondence	1849-1951	CO 368
Sessional Papers	1776-1965	CO 270
Government Gazettes	1817-1975	CO 271
Miscellanea	1819-1943	CO 272
Registers of Out-letters	1872-1926	CO 484

Tobago

after 1888 *see under* **Trinidad and Tobago**

Original Correspondence	1700-1873	CO 285
	1874-1888	CO 321
Registers of Correspondence	1850-1888	CO 376
Sessional Papers	1768-1898	CO 288
Government Gazettes	1872-1898	CO 289
Miscellanea	1766-1892	CO 290
Registers of Out-letters	1872-1882	CO 498

Trinidad and Tobago

Original Correspondence	1783-1951	CO 295
Registers of Correspondence	1850-1951	CO 372
Sessional Papers	1803-1965	CO 298
Government Gazettes	1833-1975	CO 299
Miscellanea	1804-1945	CO 300

Turks and Caicos Islands
after 1883 *see under* **Jamaica**

Original Correspondence	1799-1848	CO 23
	1848-1882	CO 301
	1878-1951	CO 137
Registers of Correspondence	1868-1882	CO 495
Sessional Papers	1849-1965	CO 303
Government Gazettes	1907-1965	CO 681
Miscellanea	1852-1947	CO 304
Registers of Out-letters	1872-1881	CO 496
	1882-1926	CO 494

Virgin Islands

Original Correspondence	1711-1872	CO 314
	1816-1853	CO 239
	1874-1951	CO 152
Registers of Correspondence	1850-1951	CO 354
Sessional Papers	1773-1965	CO 316
Miscellanea	1784-1896	CO 317
Registers of Out-letters	1872-1926	CO 507

West Indies

Original Correspondence	1624-1951	CO 318
	1948-1965	CO 1031
Registers of Correspondence	1849-1951	CO 375
Miscellanea	1820-1840	CO 320
Registers of Out-letters	1872-1926	CO 509

Windward Islands

Original Correspondence	1874-1951	CO 321
Registers of Correspondence	1850-1951	CO 376
Registers of Out-letters	1883-1926	CO 377

Appendix 2: Miscellaneous Lists

These lists have been identified from class lists and from personal research. They are not comprehensive but are intended to give an idea of the range of records available for researchers in the PRO.

Bahamas

1784   CO 23/25, f 131
Return of 52 loyalist households who arrived in the Bahamas Islands.

Barbados

1729   CO 28/21, ff 104-109, 165-209
Returns of the Negro Tax, 2/6 levy
(some duplication is found in T 1/275, ff 22-44, CO 28/40, ff 37-60, and CO 28/45, ff 107-114).

1821-1825   CO 28/97, f 108-213
Return of paupers and pensioners.

1951   CO 32/124
Electoral register.

Grenada

1763   CO 101/1, ff 18-31
Capitation Tax Rolls of people liable to pay tax on slaves.

Guyana (*formerly* British Guiana)

1764-1793   CO 116/106-117
Berbice: records of the court of policy and criminal justice [in Dutch].

1765-1794   CO 116/128-135
Berbice: Taxation returns - poll tax, church tax, etc [in Dutch].

Jamaica

1675   CO 1/35, ff 178-185
A list of His Majesty's subjects and slaves transported in HM hired ship *Hercules* from Surinam to Jamaica.

1740-1751   CO 324/55
Foreign protestants naturalized in American colonies, including Jamaica. Printed in Huguenot Society vol 24, M S Guiseppi, *Naturalization of Foreign Protestants in the American Colonies* (London, Huguenot Society, 1921).

1821-1825   CO 137/162, March
Includes a return of paupers, and a return of persons committed to the workhouse.

1831   CO 137/179
Return of persons confined to Kingston workhouse (ff 333-338), and list of negroes convicted in the parish of St Anne (f 341).

1831   CO 137/181
List of persons that have been confined in St Andrew's Workhouse claiming their freedom 1825-1831 (ff 145-148); list of convicts in the St James' Workhouse condemned to hard labour for life, 1788-1831 (f 411).

Montserrat

1716   CO 152/16, ff 148-151
Account of losses sustained in the attack by the French under Cassart in 1712.

St Christopher

1706   CO 243/2
Account of losses sustained by the proprietors and inhabitants of the island because of the invasion of the French.
(other returns in CO 152/9, ff 250-251, and CO 243/3).

St Eustatius

1781   CO 318/8, ff 83-86, 107-109
List of those appointed as Burghers between 5 Aug 1780 and 29 Jan 1781.

St Thomas

1796   FO 95/1/4, f 258
21 March 1796 includes lists of Danish subjects going to St Thomas in the West Indies.

Sierra Leone

1848   CO 267/203

Nominal list of Liberated Africans with their ages who left for Port
Antonio, Jamaica in the *Morayshire* and the *Amity Hall*.

1849   CO 267/207

Nominal list of Liberated Africans who left for St Lucia and Jamaica in the
Una, cleared Jan 1849, for Jamaica in the *Etheldred*, 29 May 1849, and for
Trinidad in the *Agnes*, 28 May 1849.

1850   CO 267/215

27 pages of petitioners, men and women, against the proposed land
and house tax.

6 pages of petitions, 385 signatories, inhabitants of Regeant, Bathurst
and Charlotte.

106 signatories in a petition by the inhabitants of Gloucester and Leicester,
comprising farmers, sawyers, journeymen carpenters, tailors, masons, etc.

Trinidad

1814-1815   CO 385/1

List of persons allowed to remain in Trinidad.

1824   CO 295/63, ff 284-285

List of freeborn men.

[missing from volume but available on film]

Appendix 3: Addresses of West Indian Archives

These addresses were taken from the *World of Learning*, 1994 edn, and from the Association of Commonwealth Archivists and Record Managers. I was unable to find archives for Dominica, Grenada and St Christopher and I have included possible contact addresses.

Antigua and Barbuda
National Archives
Long St
St John's
Antigua

Bahamas
Public Records Office
Department of Archives
POB ss-6341
Nassau
Bahamas

Barbados
Department of Archives
Black Rock
St Michael
Barbados

Belize
Belize Archives Department
26/28 Unity Blvd
Belmopan
Belize

Bermuda
Bermuda National Archives
Government Administration
Building
30 Parliament St
Hamilton HM 12
Bermuda

Cayman Islands
Cayman Islands National Archive
Goverment Administration
Building
George Town
Grand Cayman

Dominica
Documentation Dept
Government Headquarters
Roseau
Dominica

Grenada
National Museum
Young St
St George's
Grenada

Guyana
National Archives of Guyana
River Police Building
Stabroek Sqr
Georgetown
Guyana

Jamaica
Jamaica Archives
Spanish Town
Jamaica

Montserrat
Montserrat Public Library
Government Headquarters
Plymouth
Monserrat

St Christopher and Nevis
Public Library
Shirley House
Mitchell St
Basseterre
St Kitts

St Lucia
St Lucia National Archives
POB 595
Castries
St Lucia

St Vincent and the Grenadines
Department of Libraries and Archives
Kingstown
St Vincent

Trinidad and Tobago
National Archives
POB 763
St Vincent St
Port-of-Spain
Trinidad

Appendix 4: Geographical Bibliography

General texts on the West Indies

Camp, Anthony J, 'Some West Indian Sources in England', in *Family Tree Magazine*, Nov 1987, p 11.

Caribbean Historical and Genealogical Journal, TCI Genealogical Resources, PO Box 15839, San Luis, Obispo, California 93406, USA.

Dunn, Richard S, *Sugar and Slaves. The Rise of the Planter Class in the English West Indies, 1624-1713* (New York, WW Norton & Company, 1973).

Edwards, Bryan, *The History of the British West Indies*, 5th edn, 5 vols (London, 1819).

Fermor, Patrick Leigh, *The Travellers' Tree. A Journey Through the Caribbean Islands* (London,: Penguin Books, 1984).

Lawrence-Archer, Capt J H, *Monumental Inscriptions of the British West Indies* (London, Chatto and Windus, 1875).

Lucas, C P, *Historical Geography of the British Colonies, Volume 2, the West Indies* (Oxford, Clarendon Press, 1890).

Oliver, Vere Langford, ed, *Caribbeana*, 6 vols (1910-1919).

Oliver, Vere Langford, *The Monumental Inscriptions of the British West Indies* (Dorchester, The Friary Press, 1927).

Walne, Peter, ed, *A Guide to Manuscript Sources for the History of Latin America and the Caribbean in the British Isles* (Oxford University Press, 1973).

Antigua

Oliver, Vere Langford, *History of the Island of Antigua*, 3 vols (1894-1899).

Bahamas

Cash, Philip, Gordon, Shirley and Saunders, Gale, *Sources for Bahamian History* (London, MacMillan Publishing Ltd, 1991).

Craton, Michael, *A History of the Bahamas* (London, Collins, 1962).

Saunders, D, and Carson, E A, *A Guide to the Records of the Bahamas* (Nassau, 1973).

Whittleton, Eric H, 'Family History in the Bahamas', in *The Genealogists' Magazine*, vol 18, Dec 1975, pp 187-191.

Barbados

Beckles, Hilary, *A History of Barbados from Amerindian Settlement to Nation-state* (Cambridge: University Press, 1990).

Brandow, James C, *Genealogies of Barbados Families* (Baltimore,: Genealogical Publishing Co, Inc, 1983).

Chandler, M, *A Guide to Sources in Barbados* (Oxford, Basil Blackwell, 1965).

Hoyos, F A, *Barbados. A History from Amerindians to Independence* (London, MacMillan Press Ltd, 1992).

Oliver, Vere Langford, ed, *Monumental Inscriptions in Barbados* (1915).

Sanders, Joanne McRee, *Barbados Records. Baptisms 1637-1800* (Baltimore, Genealogical Publishing Co Inc, 1984).

Sanders, Joanne McRee, *Barbados Records. Marriages 1643-1800*, 2 vols (USA, Sanders Historical Publications, 1982).

Sanders, Joanne McRee, *Barbados Records. Wills and Administrations 1647-1725*, 3 vols (USA, Sanders Historical Publications, 1981).

Stanford, C J, 'Genealogical Sources in Barbados', in *The Genealogists' Magazine*, vol 17, Mar 1974, pp 489-498.

Belize

Burdon, Sir John Alder, *Archives of British Honduras*, 3 vols (London, Sifton Praed & Co Ltd, 1931).

Bolland, O Nigel, *The Formation of a Colonial Society. Belize, From Conquest to Crown Colony* (John Hopkins University Press, 1977).

Dobson, Narda, *A History of Belize* (Longman Caribbean, 1973).

Bermuda

Green, Cmdr Thomas H, *Monumental Inscriptions of The Royal Naval Cemetery, Ireland Island, Bermuda* (typescript, 1983).

Hallett, A C Hollis, *Early Bermudan Records, 1619-1826. A Guide to the Parish and Clergy Registers with some Assessment Lists and Petitions* (Bermuda, Juniperhill Press, 1991).

Hallett, C F E Hollis, *Bermuda Index, 1784-1914. An Index of Births, Marriages, and Deaths as Recorded in Bermudan Newspapers*, 2 vols (Bermuda, Juniperhill Press, 1989).

Hallett, C F E Hollis, *Early Bermuda Wills 1629-1835* (Bermuda,: Juniperhill Press, 1993).

Mercer, Julia E, *Bermuda Settlers of the 17th Century* (Baltimore, Genealogical Publishing Co, Inc, 1982).

Cayman Islands

Williams, Nigel, *A History of the Cayman Islands* (The Government of the Cayman Islands, 1970).

Grenada

Brizan, George, *Grenada. Island of Conflict. From Amerindians to People's Revolution 1498-1979* (London, Zed Books Ltd, 1984).

Jamaica

Higman, B W, *Jamaica Surveyed. Plantation Maps and Plans of the Eighteenth and Nineteenth Centuries* (Jamaica, Institute of Jamaican Publishers Ltd, 1988).

Livingston, Noel B, *Sketch Pedigrees of some of the Early Settlers in Jamaica* (Jamaica, 1909).

Soares, Charlotte, 'Jamaican Research in Britain', in *Family Tree Magazine*, Apr 1991, p 35.

Wright, Philip, 'Materials for Family History in Jamaica', in *The Genealogists' Magazine*, vol 15, Sept 1966, pp 239-250.

Wright, Philip, *Monumental Inscriptions of Jamaica* (London, Society of Genealogists, 1966).

Leeward Islands

Baker, E C, *A Guide to Records in the Leeward Islands* (Oxford, Basil Blackwell, 1965).

St Christopher

Oliver, Vere Langford, ed, *The Registers of St Thomas, Middle Island, St Kitts 1729-1832* (London, 1915).

St Lucia

Jesse, Rev C, *Outlines of St Lucia's History* (St Lucia Archaeological & Historical Society, 1964).

Sierra Leone

Fryer, Peter, *Staying Power. The History of Black People in Britain* (London, Pluto Press, 1984).

Walker, James W St G, *The Black Loyalists. The Search for a Promised Land in Nova Scotia and Sierra Leone, 1783-1870* (Longman & Dalhousie University Press, 1976).

Trinidad and Tobago

Brereton, Bridget, *A History of Modern Trindad 1783-1962* (London, Heinneman Educational Books, 1981).

Carmichael, Gertrude, *The History of the West Indian Islands of Trinidad and Tobago 1498-1900* (London, Alvin Redman Ltd, 1961).

English Protestant Church of Tobago, Register of Baptisms, Marriages and Deaths from 1781 to 1817 (Trinidad and Tobago, 1936).

Williams, Eric, *History of the People of Trinidad and Tobago* (Trinidad, PNM Publishing Co Ltd, 1961)

Virgin Islands

Dooklan, Isaac, *A History of the British Virgin Islands* (Caribbean Universities Press, 1975).

Windward Islands

Baker, E C, *A Guide to Records in the Windward Islands* (Oxford, Basil Blackwell, 1968).

INDEX

D

E

F

G